Why CESSATIONISM Can't Be True

Book 1: The Theological Perspective

Nathan J. Page

WESTBOW
PRESS®
A DIVISION OF THOMAS NELSON
& ZONDERVAN

Copyright © 2021 Nathan J. Page.

All rights reserved. No part of this book may be used or reproduced by any means, graphic, electronic, or mechanical, including photocopying, recording, taping or by any information storage retrieval system without the written permission of the author except in the case of brief quotations embodied in critical articles and reviews.

WestBow Press books may be ordered through booksellers or by contacting:

WestBow Press
A Division of Thomas Nelson & Zondervan
1663 Liberty Drive
Bloomington, IN 47403
www.westbowpress.com
844-714-3454

Because of the dynamic nature of the Internet, any web addresses or links contained in this book may have changed since publication and may no longer be valid. The views expressed in this work are solely those of the author and do not necessarily reflect the views of the publisher, and the publisher hereby disclaims any responsibility for them.

Any people depicted in stock imagery provided by Getty Images are models, and such images are being used for illustrative purposes only. Certain stock imagery © Getty Images.

Unless otherwise indicated, all Scripture taken from
the King James Version of the Bible.

Scripture quotations marked (ESV) are from the ESV® Bible (The Holy Bible, English Standard Version®), copyright © 2001 by Crossway, a publishing ministry of Good News Publishers. Used by permission. All rights reserved.

Scripture marked (ISV) taken from the Holy Bible: International Standard Version®. Copyright © 1996-forever by The ISV Foundation. ALL RIGHTS RESERVED INTERNATIONALLY. Used by permission.

ISBN: 978-1-6642-2199-4 (sc)
ISBN: 978-1-6642-2201-4 (hc)
ISBN: 978-1-6642-2200-7 (e)

Library of Congress Control Number: 2021902100

Print information available on the last page.

WestBow Press rev. date: 2/3/2021

Contents

Introduction vii
Chapter 1   Cessationist Arguments 1
Chapter 2   Arguments Refuted 10
Chapter 3   Fake Doctrine 1—Cessation of All
            Spiritual Gifts 24
Chapter 4   Fake Doctrine 2—Cessation of
            Pastors and Teachers 28
Chapter 5   Scriptural History of Signs/Sign
            Gifts 32
Chapter 6   Apostles 50
Chapter 7   Prophets and Prophecy 61
Chapter 8   Tongues 83
Chapter 9   Healing 92
Chapter 10 Miracles 98
Chapter 11 Cooperation of the Gifts 102
Chapter 12 1 Corinthians 13:8—12 106
Chapter 13 Scriptural Authority 117
Chapter 14 Commands Concerning the Gifts 119
Chapter 15 Reality Concerning the Gifts 122
Chapter 16 A Word About Visions 127
Chapter 17 Signs, Wonders, and Miracles 139
Chapter 18 Why Cessationists Are Still
            Cessationists 155
Chapter 19 It Makes a Difference 159
Conclusion 163

Introduction

I was raised in a Baptist home, being a part of a Baptist church. Out of all the "denominations" within the Church, the Baptists are one of the most devoted to doctrinal accuracy. I don't think there is any denomination that is completely sound in their theology. That is in part due to the traditions that they hold to. Almost all of the denominations have some prejudice towards biblical truth because they are resting more on their doctrinal traditions or personal experience than what the Bible actually says.

One of these doctrines is the doctrine of Cessationism. This is the belief that signs and wonders, and some of the gifts of the Holy Spirit, have ceased after the completion of the New Testament and the end of the "Apostolic Age." Many theologians and pastors (and thus the congregants as well) believe that—especially Baptists (who are usually the biggest advocates). I grew up in a Baptist church, I have been taught the Cessationist view, and I have even advocated the Cessationist view. Why? Because that is what I have been taught. Baptists are usually very Biblical in their teachings, and so I believed what was said about the "sign gifts" (as they call them). I thought it made sense, and it convinced me. Just like most people, I allowed what I grew up learning to be "the truth." I didn't ever back up for a minute and scrutinize what I believed and even defended.

When I was confronted by the statement that the Cessationist belief doesn't have one single valid scriptural support, I couldn't ignore that fact. I then began to do tremendous study on it, not to look for ways to defend what I believed, but to discover what the Scriptures actually say. After months and months of study, I couldn't grasp how twisted, inconsistent, and absurd the Cessationist doctrine and arguments were. I wrote an article that provided the basic arguments against it, but I realized that I should give the whole reality that utterly confirmed to me that Cessationism cannot be true, no matter how many logical arguments they use.

This is book 1 of *Cessationism Series*. This series is a multi-angular case against the view that the supernatural is not expected to be operated by the Church, referred to as Cessationism. In this first book, "Why Cessationism Can't Be True," I will take a theological approach. Most debates in Christian circles use this approach, but I think it is the least effective. This is merely groundwork for what lies ahead in the following books of this series.

This book (as well as the next books) is intended for pastors, theologians, and anyone who is desperate to know the actual truth. I can assure you that I am not being biased in my statements or in my conclusions. I sincerely want the truth and nothing but the truth. This is not just one of those books written by a desperate person who wants to defend his belief. It is a book that is aimed at exposing the real truth using sound handling of Scriptures.

The truth within the debate between Cessationism and Continuationism is actually very obvious and clear. Though the reasonings of both sides can make your mind perplexed and confused, only one of the sides are based on explicit Scriptural teachings. Don't focus on the reasonings and logic, even if it uses Scripture. Rather, focus on what is taught by the Bible.

The bottom line that really throws off the Cessationist doctrine is that if such a cessation occurred, it would be taught in Scripture. Instead, Cessationists use various selected verses and passages in the Bible that are not intended to teach Cessationism (whether or not it is true). The Cessationist doctrine might be defended by the Scriptures (though twisted), but it is never taught in Scripture.

I will discuss in concise detail the problems of Cessationism, and the reasons why it cannot be true. I am not simply writing why Continuationism (the opposing doctrine of Cessationism) is true, for that will not explain why the opposing doctrine can't be true. Continuationists build their case and refute the other, and yet Cessationists build their case and refute the other, and so it goes on. This really confuses people. They just cannot be assured of which belief is in fact true. I am not just writing about why Cessationism *isn't* true; I am writing why Cessationism *can't* be true. Remember, the truth cannot be completely or even mostly refuted. Truth overwhelms error. Thus, one of these opposing beliefs will confound the other, and the truth will be made clear if clearly and sincerely laid out.

1

Cessationist Arguments

In this section, I will talk like a Cessationist and defend "my" belief. I can do this because I have been immersed in it, having also been one myself. I won't be surprised if you find yourself being convinced by their arguments; however, the arguments are quite deceitful. See if you can notice what is wrong with their statements, and in the next section, I will expose them.

Disclaimer: Not all of these points are mutually accepted by Cessationists. I have brought out all the points that I have read and heard as a former Cessationist.

Though Continuationists claim that Cessationism is unbiblical, it is actually laid out very noticeably in Scripture. First, I will provide the biblical proofs of Cessationism, and then provide the other proofs.

1. The sign gifts ended when the Scriptures were completed. Paul refers to this in 1 Corinthians 13:8—12. Let's take a look at this passage:

> Charity never fails: but whether there be prophecies, they shall fail; whether there be tongues, they shall cease; whether there be knowledge, it shall vanish away. For we know in part, and we prophesy in part. But when that which is perfect is come, then that which is in part shall be done away. When I was a child, I spoke as a child, I understood as a child, I thought as a child: but when I became a man, I put away childish things. For now we see through a glass, darkly; but then face to face: now I know in part; but then shall I know even as also I am known.

This is really the only proof that is needed to prove that the sign gifts have ceased. Let's examine the passage more closely.

First of all, Paul is contrasting the permanence of love with the temporary sign gifts. Notice that Paul only mentions sign gifts: prophecy, tongues, and knowledge. These three are categories of the other sign gifts. He also says that the gifts of prophecy and knowledge will "become useless" (the literal interpretation of the Greek); whereas the gift of tongues will "cease" (the literal interpretation of the Greek).

In verse 9, Paul says that we (he and the people he is addressing) know in part and prophesy in part. They only have partial knowledge and partial prophecy (i.e. revelation). But when the perfect (i.e.

complete) comes, the partial knowledge and revelation will become useless (i.e. idle). The "perfect" must be referring to the completed Scriptures, since the Greek word for it in the Bible means "complete," which would only make sense if it were the completed Scriptures. With the Bible complete, we have all the information we need and all the revelation we need.

In verse 11, Paul explains the "perfect." He compares "childish things" with the sign gifts. "I spoke as a child" relates to the gift of tongues, "I understood as a child" relates to the gift of knowledge, and "I thought as a child" relates to the gift of prophecy. Then he says, "When I became a man, I put away childish things." Now that we have full knowledge and revelation from the completed Scriptures, we no longer need those childish gifts, which are the sign gifts.

At the time Paul was writing the epistle, they were seeing through a glass (better translated as "mirror") darkly. With the gifts of prophecy and knowledge, they can know quite a bit; however, their knowledge is still obscure and limited. But at some point, they will be able to see themselves face to face in the mirror. That mirror is the completed Scriptures. James 1:23, as well as 2 Corinthians 3:18, talks about the Bible as being a mirror.

At the time Paul was writing the epistle, they knew in part; but at some point they will know even as they are known. Again, we know he is talking about the completion of the New Testament. With the completed Scriptures, they will be able to see themselves as God sees them.

Knowing the fact that the "perfect" is referring to the completed Word of God, we know that the gifts of prophecy, tongues, and knowledge will end when the Word of God is completed. Therefore, because we do now have the completed Word, the sign gifts have already ceased.

2. Hebrews refer to sign gifts in past tense. The book of Hebrews was one of the later books written in the Bible. We see in this passage how the author and the Jews he was writing to were already looking back at the cessation of the sign gifts.

> How shall we escape, if we neglect so great salvation; which at the first began to be spoken by the Lord, and was confirmed unto us by them that heard him; God also bearing them witness, both with signs and wonders, and with divers miracles, and gifts of the Holy Ghost, according to his own will? (Hebrews 2:3—4)

Notice how he says that the message of salvation "was confirmed" by them that heard him (the Apostles) with signs and wonders, various miracles, and gifts of the Holy Spirit. "Was confirmed" is past tense. It occurred then, not at the time the author was writing Hebrews.

3. At the time John the Apostle wrote Revelation, the gift of prophecy had already ceased.

> For I testify unto every man that hears the words of the prophecy of this book, If any man shall add unto these things, God shall add unto him the plagues that are written in this book. (Revelation 22:18)

John says that whoever adds to the prophecies written in Scripture will be plagued by God of the plagues written in the Scriptures. This is serious, and we are warned not to prophesy.

4. Apostles and prophets were foundational to the Church.

> Now therefore ye are no more strangers and foreigners, but fellowcitizens with the saints, and of the household of God; And are built upon the foundation of the apostles and prophets, Jesus Christ himself being the chief corner stone. (Ephesians 2:19—20)

Apostles and prophets are no longer around today. Those offices were strictly for those in the infant days of the Church. They are foundational, and we cannot continue to lay the foundation, but proceed with the building.

5. The sign gifts were given to confirm the message that was being preached. Mark 16:20 affirms this:

> And they went forth, and preached everywhere, the Lord working with them, and confirming the word with signs following.

The Scriptures were not completed yet, so the apostles needed signs to validate the message. Now that the Word of God is complete, there is no more need for confirmation, since it is already part of the Scriptures.

6. The sign gifts were mainly for the Apostles to validate their authority. Second Corinthians 12:12 says,

> Truly the signs of an apostle were wrought among you in all patience, in signs, and wonders, and mighty deeds.

Because the office of apostleship ceased, it is no doubt that the sign gifts that accompanied them ceased as well. Apostles and their sign gifts were all foundational to the establishing of the Church. They were like the formula for a baby. Now that the Church is not in its infant stage, there is no need for the formula.

7. The sign gifts were for the Jews, to reveal to them the fulfilled prophecies concerning the Messiah and the Church. The gift of tongues served as a sign of judgment to them according to 1 Corinthians 14:21—22:

> In the law it is written, With men of other tongues and other lips will I speak unto this people; and yet for all that will they not hear me, saith the Lord. Wherefore tongues are for a sign, not to them that believe, but to them that believe not.

The Apostles were Jews, and with the signs gifts came the realization of the beginning of the church age. The other Jews were given those signs done by the Apostles, but they still did not believe. With that unbelief came the judgment. Jesus spoke to them in parables; the Apostles spoke to them in tongues that could not be understood. Finally their temple was destroyed, marking the end of all prior signs of judgment.

8. It is not difficult at all to see the dying out of the sign gifts in the New Testament. The book of 1 Corinthians (one of the earlier epistles written) mentioned a lot about the gifts. However, the later epistles either didn't mention any of the gifts, or only mentioned fewer of them. This is the chronological order in which the epistles that mention the gifts of the Spirit are written: 1 Corinthians, Romans, Ephesians, and 1 Peter.

1 Corinthians mentioned all of the sign gifts: apostles, prophets, wisdom, knowledge, discernment of spirits, miracles, healings, tongues, and interpretation of tongues. Romans only mentioned one sign gift: prophecy. Ephesians mentioned only two: apostles and prophets. 1 Peter didn't mention any of the sign gifts.

As the epistles were being written, the sign gifts were gradually ceasing. In Ephesians, apostles and prophets were only mentioned as foundational (as was told previously in the epistle, in chapter 2, verse 20). As is clearly seen, when the Church began to grow and mature, the foundational sign gifts began to diminish. In his later epistles (1 Timothy, 2 Timothy, and Philippians), Paul did not heal those who were sick. Instead of healing Timothy, Paul told him to take a little wine as treatment for his illnesses (1 Timothy 5:23). Instead of healing Trophimus, Paul left him sick at Miletus (2 Timothy 4:20). When Epaphroditus was sick, even near the point of death, Paul didn't heal him (Philippians 2:26—27). He didn't heal because he couldn't do so.

9. In addition to the diminishing of the sign gifts as according to the New Testament, we can see according to history that the sign gifts began to diminish. After the Apostles were gone, there was suddenly no such record of people speaking in tongues, healing people, or performing miracles. Only until more recently have people claimed to have such gifts.

In the Apostolic Age, the sign gifts were being performed by many constantly; however, that suddenly changed at the end of the Apostolic Age. It is clear that those gifts had ceased, or else there would be some consistent mentioning of them in historical accounts of the Church and the Church fathers.

10. There are so many problems and abuses that occur within churches that claim to use these sign gifts. Speaking in tongues causes chaos in the churches, prophecies end up false and unfulfilled, demons don't get cast out of possessed people, people don't really get healed by "faith healers," and people don't get raised from the dead.

How can there really be sign gifts given today if they are always associated with problems? It doesn't take long to notice the phoniness of these "gifts". Why are there always problems in the church when sign gifts are introduced into it? The simple answer is that they are not genuine. The sign gifts have ceased to be given a long time ago.

11. A significant point that is worth mentioning is the fact that many of the Church fathers believed this. Additionally, many Church fathers have never recorded that sign gifts were still around or claimed to possess any of the sign gifts.

12. The last point that I will mention is that God no longer works in the outward; He only works in the inward. In the infant days of the Church, sign gifts were given to show that God was now working in the inward through the Word of God and the Spirit of God. The Apostolic Age was a transition period between working in the outward and working in the inward.

False prophets work in the outward appearance, using signs and wonders to deceive. Matthew 24:24 says,

> For there shall arise false Christs, and false prophets, and shall shew great signs and wonders; insomuch that, if it were possible, they shall deceive the very elect.

Using signs is a distraction. That is why we must only give the Gospel and the truth, and let the Holy Spirit work. Using signs is placing the emphasis on us and not on God. It is also distracting others from the work of the Spirit.

2

Arguments Refuted

The arguments in the previous section can be quite convincing if not examined carefully. Many people are naïve, and just take what teachers of Cessationism say to backup what they teach as adequate and true. We must, however, check what is said with Scripture and reality. Those arguments I mentioned in the previous section are very faulty, and I will show you in this section how they are. To do this, I will insert my comments within the points being made.

1. The sign gifts ended when the Scriptures were completed. *Paul refers to this in 1 Corinthians 13:8—12. Let's take a look at this passage:*

> *Charity never fails: but whether there be prophecies, they shall fail; whether there be tongues, they shall cease; whether there be knowledge, it shall vanish away. For we know in part, and we prophesy in part. But when that which is perfect is come, then that which is in part shall be done away. When I was a child, I*

spoke as a child, I understood as a child, I thought as a child: but when I became a man, I put away childish things. For now we see through a glass, darkly; but then face to face: now I know in part; but then shall I know even as also I am known.

This is really the only proof that is needed to prove that the sign gifts have ceased. Let's examine the passage more closely.

First of all, Paul is contrasting the permanence of love with the temporary sign gifts. Notice that Paul only mentions sign gifts: prophecy, tongues, and knowledge. [He doesn't mention all of the sign gifts though. Also, the term "sign gifts" was invented by man.] *These three are categories of the other sign gifts.* [Really? How do you know that? Not all of the sign gifts fit into any of those categories very well, such as the gift of working miracles.] *He also says that the gifts of prophecy and knowledge will "become useless" (the literal interpretation of the Greek); whereas the gift of tongues will "cease" (the literal interpretation of the Greek).*

In verse 9, Paul says that we (he and the people he is addressing) know in part and prophesy in part. [Paul certainly had tremendous knowledge. As a matter of fact, we get most of the New Testament from his writings. He said that even he only knows in part. Do we know more than Paul because we have the New Testament? Remember, he is the one who wrote most of it, and he said that he only knew in part. I certainly don't know more than Paul knew, even though I have the completed Word of God; so certainly, I also only know in part—and less than that of Paul who also only knew in part.] *They only have partial knowledge and partial prophecy (i.e. revelation). But when the perfect (i.e. complete) comes, the partial knowledge and revelation will become useless (i.e. idle). The "perfect" must be referring to the completed Scriptures, since the Greek word for it in the Bible means "complete," which would only make sense if it were the completed Scriptures.* [How can you know? Why would Paul be so vague in referring to the completion of Scripture by just saying "the perfect"? How would the Corinthians have known he was talking about the completion of Scripture? Any time an author of a book of the Bible wanted to refer to the Scriptures, they used explicit words that clearly referred to the Scriptures.] *With the Bible complete, we have all the information we need and all the revelation we need.* [But our knowledge and revelation is still incomplete and in part. Paul said that "now" "we" know in part and prophecy in part. We still today, even with the complete Word of God, have only partial knowledge and revelation.]

In verse 11, Paul explains the "perfect." He compares "childish things" with the sign gifts. "I spoke as a child" relates to the gift of tongues, "I understood as a child" relates to the gift of knowledge, and "I thought as a child" relates to the gift of prophecy. Then he says, "When I became a man, I put away childish things." Now that we have full knowledge and revelation from the completed Scriptures, we no longer need those childish gifts, which are the sign gifts. [But when are the childish things put away, as according to Paul? It is when he becomes a man. The childish things are referring to the sign gifts, you say, and he (the "I") had those sign gifts/childish things. But then you change the "I" from Paul to the Scriptures, as I see it

Why Cessationism Can't Be True

in your reasonings. Do the Scriptures put away the childish things (sign gifts) when it is completed? Did the Scriptures possess those childish things? When are the sign gifts/childish things put away? They are put away when Paul becomes a man. Verse 10 says that the gifts are put away when the perfect comes; verse 11 says that the sign gifts are put away when the person becomes spiritually mature. How could that be referring to the completion of Scripture?]

At the time Paul was writing the epistle, they were seeing through a glass (better translated as "mirror") darkly. With the gifts of prophecy and knowledge, they can know quite a bit; however, their knowledge is still obscure and limited. But at some point, they will be able to see themselves face to face in the mirror. That mirror is the completed Scriptures. [First Corinthians 13:8—12 does not refer to the incompletion and completion of Scripture; rather, it refers to the incompletion and completion of our knowledge and revelation. You are using inconsistent logic by referring to the incompletion of our knowledge and revelation, and then referring to the completion of the Scriptures.] *James 1:23, as well as 2 Corinthians 3:18, talks about the Bible as being a mirror.* [They also don't just say "mirror," but also clarify what is being alluded to. The big problem with this reasoning though, is that those texts were written after this was written, which means that the Corinthians reading this would not have those texts to relate "the perfect" or "mirror/ glass" to. So how would they conclude that the completion of Scripture was what Paul meant by "the perfect"?]

At the time Paul was writing the epistle, they knew in part; but at some point they will know even as they are known. [Known of whom? It could only be referring to God. Do you know as much as you are known by God? Certainly not!] *Again, we know he is talking about the completion of the New Testament. With the completed Scriptures, they will be able to see themselves as God sees them.* [That is not what it said. It said we will "know" as God "knows" us, not "see" as God "sees" us.]

Knowing the fact that the "perfect" is referring to the completed Word of God, we know that the gifts of prophecy, tongues, and knowledge will end when the Word of God is completed. Therefore, because we do now have the completed Word, the sign gifts have already ceased.

2. Hebrews refer to sign gifts in past tense. *The book of Hebrews was one of the later books written in the Bible. We see in this passage how the author and the Jews he was writing to were already looking back at the cessation of the sign gifts.*

> *How shall we escape, if we neglect so great salvation; which at the first began to be spoken by the Lord, and was confirmed unto us by them that heard him; God also bearing them witness, both with signs and wonders, and with divers miracles, and gifts of the Holy Ghost, according to his own will? (Hebrews 2:3—4)*

Notice how he says that the message of salvation "was confirmed" by them that heard him (the Apostles) with signs and wonders, various miracles, and gifts of the Holy Spirit. "Was confirmed" is past tense. It occurred then, not at the time the author was writing

Why Cessationism Can't Be True

Hebrews. [How does the past tense mean it never happens in the present? If I say that I was paid my salary by my employer, does that mean that I don't get paid anymore, since I am saying it in past tense? Not at all! If I say that I ate pizza last Friday, does that mean that I don't eat pizza anymore? When the author of Hebrews said that the message was confirmed, he was referring specifically to the people he was writing to. He was talking about the confirmation made to them in specific, so of course it was in the past. They don't need another confirmation; only other people and newer generations need confirmation.]

3. At the time John the Apostle wrote Revelation, the gift of prophecy had already ceased.

> *For I testify unto every man that hears the words of the prophecy of this book, If any man shall add unto these things, God shall add unto him the plagues that are written in this book. (Revelation 22:18)*

John says that whoever adds to the prophecies written in Scripture will be plagued by God of the plagues written in the Scriptures. This is serious, and we are warned not to prophesy. [Not whoever prophesies. It is whoever prophesies and then adds it to what John is saying. It is okay to prophesy; it is not okay to add it the book of Revelation (or at most, the Scriptures). He says that whoever adds to *these* things (these prophecies), God shall add unto him the plagues that are written in this book (the book of Revelation).]

4. Apostles and prophets were foundational to the Church.

> Now therefore ye are no more strangers and foreigners, but fellowcitizens with the saints, and of the household of God; And are built upon the foundation of the apostles and prophets, Jesus Christ himself being the chief corner stone. (Ephesians 2:19—20)

Apostles and prophets are no longer around today. Those offices were strictly for those in the infant days of the Church. They are foundational, and we cannot continue to lay the foundation, but proceed with the building. [The apostles and prophets were not the foundation itself; they laid the foundation. The foundation of the house is not the house itself. The foundation of the apostles and prophets is not the apostles and prophets themselves; rather, it is a foundation that was laid by the apostles and prophets (according to 1 Corinthians 3:10—11). The foundation of Jesus Christ continues to be laid by apostles and prophets as the Gospel advances in regions and generations that have not yet been reached.]

5. The sign gifts were given to confirm the message that was being preached. Mark 16:20 affirms this:

> And they went forth, and preached everywhere, the Lord working with them, and confirming the word with signs following.

The Scriptures were not completed yet, so the apostles needed signs to validate the message. [Aren't we still confirming the message today? I don't think everyone believes that the message of Christ is true, so we still need to confirm what we preach.] *Now that the Word of God is complete, there is no more need for confirmation, since it is already part of the Scriptures.* [Says who? Of course there is still need to confirm the Gospel message, and the Holy Spirit is the one who does that.]

6. *The sign gifts were mainly for the Apostles to validate their authority.* [It wasn't only for the validation of apostolic authority, however. Agabus and Philipp's four daughters were not apostles, yet they had the gift of prophecy. Many Gentiles spoke in tongues, though they were not apostles. Stephen was not an apostle, and yet performed signs and wonders. And, there are still apostles today as will be discussed later on.] *Second Corinthians 12:12 says,*

> *Truly the signs of an apostle were wrought among you in all patience, in signs, and wonders, and mighty deeds.*

Because the office of apostleship ceased, it is no doubt that the sign gifts that accompanied them ceased as well. [The office of apostleship did not cease.] *Apostles and their sign gifts were all foundational to the establishing of the Church. They were like the formula for a baby. Now that the Church is not in its infant stage, there is no need for the formula.* [It is more like the Twelve Apostles that were the formula for the infant Church. Today's apostles are the milk for the growing Church. The Twelve Apostles (the formula) were somewhat different than today's apostles (the milk), so to give a special solid stability to the infant Church. The milk is not relied on as much as the formula was, but it is still important.]

7. The sign gifts were for the Jews, to reveal to them the fulfilled prophecies concerning the Messiah and the Church. [Aren't there still Jews today?] *The gift of tongues served as a sign of judgment to them according to 1 Corinthians 14:21—22:*

> *In the law it is written, With men of other tongues and other lips will I speak unto this people; and yet for all that will they not hear me, saith the Lord. Wherefore tongues are for a sign, not to them that believe, but to them that believe not.*

The Apostles were Jews, and with the signs gifts came the realization of the beginning of the Church age. [That was one purpose of the signs and "sign gifts."] *The other Jews were given those signs done by the Apostles, but they still did not believe. With that unbelief came the judgment. Jesus spoke to them in parables; the Apostles spoke to them in tongues that could not be understood. Finally their temple was destroyed, marking the end of all prior signs of judgment.* [How do you know that the temple's destruction marked the end of judgment upon the Jews? Is that what God said? The Jews are still being judged, and the kingdom is still being revealed to them by signs, and it will be until after the Day of the Lord.]

8. It is not difficult at all to see the dying out of the sign gifts in the New Testament. *The book* *of 1 Corinthians (one of the earlier epistles written) mentioned a lot about the gifts. However, the later epistles either didn't mention any of the gifts, or only mentioned fewer of them.* [What proof does that offer? That is only a subject of bias observation.] *This is the chronological order in which the epistles that mention the gifts of the Spirit are written: 1 Corinthians, Romans, Ephesians, and 1 Peter.*

1 Corinthians mentioned all of the sign gifts: apostles, prophets, wisdom, knowledge, discernment of spirits, miracles, healings, tongues, and interpretation of tongues. Romans only mentioned one sign gift: prophecy. Ephesians mentioned only two: apostles and prophets. 1 Peter didn't mention any of the sign gifts. [Notice also that there are sign gifts and gifts added to the lists and taken away; even the gifts that are agreed upon to not have ceased are seen to not be mentioned in the later books. The reasoning that was used is inconsistent with the other gifts.]
As the epistles were being written, the sign gifts were gradually ceasing. In Ephesians, apostles and prophets were only mentioned as foundational (as was told previously in the epistle, in chapter 2, verse 20). [Not true!] *As is clearly seen, when the Church began to grow and mature, the foundational sign gifts began to diminish.* [They didn't cease. There were still people that were given sign gifts.] *In his later epistles (1 Timothy, 2 Timothy, and Philippians), Paul did not heal those who were sick. Instead of healing Timothy, Paul told him to take a little wine as treatment for his illnesses (1 Timothy 5:23).* [Paul was not with Timothy to lay hands on him.] *Instead of healing Trophimus, Paul left him sick at Miletus (2 Timothy 4:20). When*

Epaphroditus was sick, even near the point of death, Paul didn't heal him (Philippians 2:26—27). He didn't heal because he couldn't do so. [But Epaphroditus did get healed ("but God had mercy on him") and was able to go to Philippi. Acts 28:8 mentions Paul healing Publius' father and may sick folks on Malta. This was right at the time the book of Philippians was written; thus, he didn't lose his gift.]

9. In addition to the diminishing of the sign gifts as according to the New Testament, we can see according to history that the sign gifts began to diminish. *After the Apostles were gone, there was suddenly no such record of people speaking in tongues, healing people, or performing miracles. Only until more recently have people claimed to have such gifts.* [If it did begin to diminish, it still did not cease. Just because it became uncommon does not mean it ceased. It only means it became uncommon. There are many factors that would play into this. Just because there were no records (but there were records), that does not mean it did not occur. The gifts being used were not an emphasis in the written records. For example, you don't find the gift of mercy recorded in historical writings; but that was and is still being given by the Spirit. Nonetheless, there has been many records of signs being done, even after the Scriptures were completed. You are probably just not aware of these records.]

In the Apostolic Age, the sign gifts were being performed by many constantly; however, that suddenly changed at the end of the Apostolic Age. It is clear that those gifts had ceased, or else there would be some consistent mentioning of them in historical accounts of

Why Cessationism Can't Be True

the Church and the Church fathers. [Not true. There was no mentioning of anybody breathing. Does that mean they ceased to breath? No! Just because they didn't mention any sign gifts being used (they didn't mention many "normal" gifts either), that does not mean it ceased. Simply put, they did not focus on the gifts that were being exercised, especially the "smaller" gifts, such as the gift of knowledge, the gift of wisdom, and the gift of discernment.]

10. There are so many problems and abuses that occur within churches that claim to use these sign gifts. [Just because problems are associated with the gifts doesn't mean that the gifts aren't genuine. There were the same problems in the Corinthian church, yet those gifts were genuine.] *Speaking in tongues causes chaos in the churches, prophecies end up false and unfulfilled, demons don't get cast out of possessed people, people don't really get healed by "faith healers," and people don't get raised from the dead.* [Some information is missing. Speaking in tongues doesn't always cause chaos, not all prophecies turn out to be false, demons do get cast out, people do get healed by the laying on of hands, and there have been people who have been raised from the dead.]

How can there really be sign gifts given today if they are always associated with problems? [There are not always problems.] *It doesn't take long to notice the phoniness of these "gifts". Why are there always problems in the church when sign gifts are introduced into it? The simple answer is that they are not genuine. The sign gifts have ceased to be given a long time ago.* [There are indeed counterfeits, but there are also genuine gifts.]

11. A significant point that is worth mentioning is the fact that many of the Church fathers believed this. [Humans are prone to error. Just because these expert theologians believed in Cessationism, it doesn't mean that Cessationism is true. There were preachers and teachers in Jerusalem who believed and taught that circumcision was part of salvation (Acts 15:1, 24).] *Additionally, many Church fathers have never recorded that sign gifts were still around or claimed to possess any of the sign gifts.* [But not all of the Church fathers never claimed to possess any of these gifts. One such example is Saint Patrick of Ireland, who had the gift of prophecy. He prophesied of even the month and year when his prophecy would be fulfilled, and all his prophecies were fulfilled. The same is true of John Knox and George Wishart. Just because something wasn't recorded doesn't mean it didn't happen.]

12. The last point that I will mention is that God no longer works in the outward; He only works in the inward. [Nowhere in the Bible does it say that!] *In the infant days of the Church, sign gifts were given to show that God was now working in the inward through the Word of God and the Spirit of God.* [Is that what the Bible says? See Mark 16:20, Hebrews 2:4, and Romans 15:18—19. Where in the Bible does it say that the signs and sign gifts were given to show that God was now working in the inward?] *The Apostolic Age was a transition period between working in the outward and working in the inward.* [The transition period was when John the Baptist and Jesus the Messiah were on the earth, and that was a transition between the Old Testament and the New Testament.]

False prophets work in the outward appearance, using signs and wonders to deceive. [Then why were the Apostles using signs? There were false prophets and apostles then at that time.] *Matthew 24:24 says,*

> *For there shall arise false Christs, and false prophets, and shall shew great signs and wonders; insomuch that, if it were possible, they shall deceive the very elect.*

Using signs is a distraction. That is why we must only give the Gospel and the truth, and let the Holy Spirit work. [The signs are works of the Spirit.] *Using signs is placing the emphasis on us and not on God. It is also distracting others from the work of the Spirit.* [That is if we give ourselves the credit. However, we must instead give God the credit (2 Corinthians 10:17—18, 1 Corinthians 4:7).]

3

Fake Doctrine 1—Cessation of All Spiritual Gifts

In order to get the Cessationists out there to realize the faultiness and inconsistency of their reasoning, I think it would be effective to use their reasoning to support doctrines that I hope we all agree aren't true. Don't think I hold onto these beliefs, because I don't. The first "fake doctrine" is the cessation of all spiritual gifts. Instead of just saying that the sign gifts ceased after the Apostolic Age, we should say that all of the gifts of the Spirit ceased; after all, there are only a few gifts left. If we use the reasoning used by Cessationists to support their view, we would have to conclude that all of the gifts of the Spirit were only for the infant days of the Church and have therefore ceased to be given to believers today. Let me present the evidences for the cessation of all spiritual gifts.

The first is that we can see the fading away of these gifts throughout the New Testament, from the first epistles written to the later epistles written. From the first epistles that deal with the gifts of the Spirit to the

Why Cessationism Can't Be True

last ones, we have 1 Corinthians, Romans, Ephesians, and 1 Peter. In 1 Corinthians, we have the gifts of apostles, prophets, teachers, wisdom, knowledge, faith, healings, miracles, discerning of spirits, tongues, interpretation of tongues, helps, and governments. In Romans, we have the gifts of prophecy, teachers, ministry, exhortation, giving, ruling, and mercy.

By the time Romans was written, apostles were no more being added to the Church, and the gifts of wisdom, knowledge, faith, healings, miracles, discerning of spirits, tongues, interpretation of tongues, helps, and governments had already ceased to be given. In Ephesians and 1 Peter (they were written in around the same time), we have the offices of apostles and prophets as foundational (the gifts are them as in the writings of Scripture), evangelists, pastor-teachers, speaking, and ministry. During that time, the gifts of prophecy, exhortation, giving, ruling, and mercy had already ceased. The gifts that are left are evangelists, pastor-teachers, speaking, and ministry; the other gifts had already ceased. Of course after those books we have no such gifts being listed anymore.

The second evidence is that we can see the diminishing of these gifts by looking at the history of the Church. After the Apostolic Age, there hasn't been much prophesying, and the prophecies that were prophesied turned out to be false (as we also see today). Wisdom now comes from the Word of God, not directly from the Spirit of God; that's why those who do not read much of God's Word make foolish choices and are not wise. Without reading Scripture, no one can have knowledge of spiritual things. Even when we do read the Scriptures, we have trouble interpreting it. Who has the faith to remove mountains anymore?

We all don't have as much faith that the Apostles had; that's because they had a special gift of faith. Why don't anybody empty out hospitals and prevent Christians from having to go to the doctor's by healing them? It is because nobody has that gift. Miracles aren't being performed by people as the Apostles did in the beginning years of the Church.

Do you know anybody who can discern between spirits without the use of God's Word? Probably not, because that gift does not exist (despite the claims some may make). No one in earlier Church history after the Apostolic Age mentioned or claimed the use of the gift of tongues or interpretation of tongues. Only until recently have people claimed to have such gifts. How many churches have people who exhort one another? Not many! In Acts and the earlier epistles, we see how generous the believers were. They would give all that they have, selling their property and possessions to give to the churches. We don't have that anymore! Otherwise, poverty would be wiped away from the earth by now. Can you see the diminishing of these gifts throughout history? I can!

Third, all the gifts of the Spirit were outward, and were given as a boost to the infant Church because the Scriptures were not completed, and thus, there was a need for extra-biblical gifts. One example is the gift of exhortation. Hebrews 10 gives the command for believers to exhort each other. But before that was written, there was no scriptural revelation about the need to exhort one another in the Church. That's why God gave certain believers the gift of exhortation—to allow there to be exhortation before the Scriptures revealed the need.

The gift of the word of wisdom has also ceased

Why Cessationism Can't Be True

because it was needed prior to the completion of Scripture. We have all the wisdom we need through God's Word (2 Timothy 3:15—17, Psalm 19:7), so the need for a gift of wisdom is unnecessary.

Let the word of Christ dwell in you richly in all wisdom; teaching and admonishing one another in psalms and hymns and spiritual songs, singing with grace in your hearts to the Lord. (Colossians 3:16)

The same thing can be applied to the gifts of knowledge, prophecy, teaching, discernment, generosity, service, and most of the other gifts. Basically, the gifts were given as an aid to the infant Church, and were foundational to the rest of the building.

These three significant evidences demonstrate the obviousness of the fact that the gifts given by the Holy Spirit have ceased after the Apostolic Age of the Church. Now, we rely on the Word of God, which is the ultimate gift given as a replacement of the personal spiritual gifts. And, of course, the Holy Spirit is another gift that will aid us in improving.

4

Fake Doctrine 2—Cessation of Pastors and Teachers

The second "fake doctrine" I will introduce is the cessation of pastors and teachers. How can I ever come up with that idea? Easy, if I use the logic Cessationists use! Once the Scriptures were completed, there was no more need for pastors and teachers; thus, those offices ceased to be given by the Spirit. There are a few evidences that prove this belief.

The first is found in 2 Timothy 3:15—17:

> And that from a child thou hast known the holy scriptures, which are able to make thee wise unto salvation through faith which is in Christ Jesus. All scripture is given by inspiration of God, and is profitable for doctrine, for reproof, for correction, for instruction in righteousness: That the man of God may be perfect, throughly furnished unto all good works.

Why Cessationism Can't Be True

With the Word of God, we have the Gospel and the way of salvation, doctrine, reproof, correction, and instruction for practical living. Through the Word of God, we can be spiritually mature, fully equipped for doing good works.

Second Timothy was one of the later epistles written, and it never mentioned the office of pastors or teachers. Instead, it says that the Scriptures are the source of doctrine and instruction. The epistles written after it (e.g. 1 John, 2 John, 3 John, Jude, and Revelation) never mentioned pastors or teachers in regards to them still functioning, either. That is because they have ceased to be offices. They were given because there was not very much information in the Scriptures. The teachings and instructions came from Christ to the early Apostles. They in turn gave the teachings and instructions to the pastors and teachers, who gave the teachings and instructions to the other believers. With the Word of God completed, every believer has access to the teachings and instructions of Christ.

The second evidence is found in another later epistle that was written, which is 1 John 2:27.

> But the anointing which ye have received of him abideth in you, and ye need not that any man teach you: but as the same anointing teacheth you of all things, and is truth, and is no lie, and even as it hath taught you, ye shall abide in him.

Remember that it is the Spirit who wields the Word of God (Ephesians 6:17). Now that it is fully complete, the Spirit can now reveal the truths and instructions of God through it. John literally says that we do not need man to teach us anymore. We have the Spirit to teach us all things pertaining to Christianity. Of course, it is unleashed through the utilizing of the sword of the Spirit, which is the Word of God.

The third evidence which I have mentioned previously is that we can see the ceasing of the offices as we look throughout the New Testament, from the earlier epistles to the later epistles. They were mentioned a lot in the earlier epistles (such as 1 Corinthians, Ephesians, Titus, Philippians, James, Hebrews, and 1 Peter), but in the later epistles (2 Timothy, 1 John, 2 John, 3 John, Jude, and Revelation) they were never mentioned in reference to them still being around. It is quite obvious then—in addition to the preceding two points—that those offices have ceased to function.

The fourth evidence is that there have been many problems associated with the offices of pastors and teachers. There are so many false teachers (2 Peter 2:1—3) in the world. They teach for financial gain and they preach for popularity gain. But another problem is that even sincere pastors and teachers may end up teaching erroneous teachings to others. It is only safe to find truth through the Scriptures. Humans are humans—prone to error. You can't know for certain if they are preaching and teaching the truth. Why are there so many disagreements and opposing beliefs among pastors and teachers? And what problem did that cause? It caused the Church to split into denominations. Instead of uniting together over the Word of Truth, they split up over differing beliefs among pastors and teachers.

> Now this I say, that every one of you saith, I am of Paul; and I of Apollos; and I of Cephas; and I of Christ. Is Christ divided? (1 Corinthians 1:12—13a)

> For ye are yet carnal: for whereas there is among you envying, and strife, and divisions, are ye not carnal, and walk as men? For while one saith, I am of Paul; and another, I am of Apollos; are ye not carnal? (1 Corinthians 3:3—4)

This is exactly what is happening now, but to a far greater extent, all because there are pastors and teachers when there shouldn't be any.

Churches should be coming together for fellowship and provoking one another to good works (Hebrews 10:24—25), guided under the reading and studying of God's Word, and focused on the Gospel of Christ (Philippians 1:27). The church is not meant to be a place of sitting under the teachings of a pastor or teacher, naïvely believing what they say, and leaving to do the daily activities. It is meant to be a place of spiritual fellowship and mutual encouragement, studying God's Word together, and provoking each other to further evangelize the world. With the Word of God complete, we don't need to rely on fourth-hand teachers, fifth-hand teachers, sixth-hand teachers, etc. to give us the truth. We have the complete Word of God, which came from God. There is no such more accurate source than the perfect Scriptures of God.

5

Scriptural History of Signs/Sign Gifts

In this section, we will review the timeline of the existence of the sign gifts as mentioned in the New Testament Scriptures. We will do this to see if there really was an end to these gifts implied according to the mentioning of it in Scripture (as Cessationists claim). I will go through the apostolic timeline (A.D. 30—A.D. 95) and give mostly all (I tried as best as I could) of the passages in the New Testament that imply that the gifts were occurring at the time they were written.

A.D. 30

> And these signs shall follow them that believe; In my name shall they cast out devils; they shall speak with new tongues; They shall take up serpents; and if they drink any deadly thing, it shall not hurt them; they shall lay hands on the sick, and they shall recover. (Mark 16:17—18)

And they went forth, and preached everywhere, the Lord working with them, and confirming the word with signs following. Amen. (Mark 16:20)

And when the day of Pentecost was fully come, they were all with one accord in one place. And suddenly there came a sound from heaven as of a rushing mighty wind, and it filled all the house where they were sitting. And there appeared unto them cloven tongues like as of fire, and it sat upon each of them. And they were all filled with the Holy Ghost, and began to speak with other tongues, as the Spirit gave them utterance.

And there were dwelling at Jerusalem Jews, devout men, out of every nation under heaven. Now when this was noised abroad, the multitude came together, and were confounded, because that every man heard them speak in his own language. And they were all amazed and marvelled, saying one to another, Behold, are not all these which speak Galilaeans? And how hear we every man in our own tongue, wherein we were born? Parthians, and Medes, and Elamites, and the dwellers in Mesopotamia, and in Judaea, and Cappadocia, in Pontus, and Asia, Phrygia, and Pamphylia, in Egypt, and in the parts of Libya about Cyrene, and strangers of Rome, Jews and proselytes,

Cretes and Arabians, we do hear them speak in our tongues the wonderful works of God. And they were all amazed, and were in doubt, saying one to another, What meaneth this? Others mocking said, These men are full of new wine.

But Peter, standing up with the eleven, lifted up his voice, and said unto them, Ye men of Judaea, and all ye that dwell at Jerusalem, be this known unto you, and hearken to my words: For these are not drunken, as ye suppose, seeing it is but the third hour of the day. But this is that which was spoken by the prophet Joel; And it shall come to pass in the last days, saith God, I will pour out of my Spirit upon all flesh: and your sons and your daughters shall prophesy, and your young men shall see visions, and your old men shall dream dreams: And on my servants and on my handmaidens I will pour out in those days of my Spirit; and they shall prophesy: And I will shew wonders in heaven above, and signs in the earth beneath; blood, and fire, and vapour of smoke: The sun shall be turned into darkness, and the moon into blood, before that great and notable day of the Lord come: And it shall come to pass, that whosoever shall call on the name of the Lord shall be saved. (Acts 2:1—21)

And fear came upon every soul: and many wonders and signs were done by the apostles. (Acts 2:43)

And as the lame man which was healed held Peter and John, all the people ran together unto them in the porch that is called Solomon's, greatly wondering. (Acts 3:11)

And beholding the man which was healed standing with them, they could say nothing against it. (Acts 4:14)

Saying, What shall we do to these men? for that indeed a notable miracle hath been done by them is manifest to all them that dwell in Jerusalem; and we cannot deny it. (Acts 4:16)

By stretching forth thine hand to heal; and that signs and wonders may be done by the name of thy holy child Jesus. (Acts 4:30)

And by the hands of the apostles were many signs and wonders wrought among the people; (and they were all with one accord in Solomon's porch. (Acts 5:12)

There came also a multitude out of the cities round about unto Jerusalem, bringing sick folks, and them which were vexed with unclean spirits: and they were healed every one. (Acts 5:16)

And Stephen, full of faith and power, did great wonders and miracles among the people. (Acts 6:8)

And the people with one accord gave heed unto those things which Philip spake, hearing and seeing the miracles which he did. For unclean spirits, crying with loud voice, came out of many that were possessed with them: and many taken with palsies, and that were lame, were healed. (Acts 8:6—7)

Then Simon himself believed also: and when he was baptized, he continued with Philip, and wondered, beholding the miracles and signs which were done. (Acts 8:13)

For they heard them speak with tongues, and magnify God. (Acts 10:46)

A.D. 40

And in these days came prophets from Jerusalem unto Antioch. (Acts 11:27)

Now there were in the church that was at Antioch certain prophets and teachers; as Barnabas, and Simeon that was called Niger, and Lucius of Cyrene, and

Manaen, which had been brought up with Herod the tetrarch, and Saul. (Acts 13:1)

Long time therefore abode they speaking boldly in the Lord, which gave testimony unto the word of his grace, and granted signs and wonders to be done by their hands. (Acts 14:3)

The same heard Paul speak: who stedfastly beholding him, and perceiving that he had faith to be healed, Said with a loud voice, Stand upright on thy feet. And he leaped and walked. (Acts 14:9—10)

Then all the multitude kept silence, and gave audience to Barnabas and Paul, declaring what miracles and wonders God had wrought among the Gentiles by them. (Acts 15:12)

And they wrote letters by them after this manner; The apostles and elders and brethren send greeting unto the brethren which are of the Gentiles in Antioch and Syria and Cilicia. (Acts 15:23)

And Judas and Silas, being prophets also themselves, exhorted the brethren with many words, and confirmed them. (Acts 15:32)

And as they went through the cities, they delivered them the decrees for to keep, that were ordained of the apostles and elders which were at Jerusalem. (Acts 16:4)

Take, my brethren, the prophets, who have spoken in the name of the Lord, for an example of suffering affliction, and of patience. (James 5:10)

Is any sick among you? let him call for the elders of the church; and let them pray over him, anointing him with oil in the name of the Lord: And the prayer of faith shall save the sick, and the Lord shall raise him up; and if he have committed sins, they shall be forgiven him. Confess your faults one to another, and pray one for another, that ye may be healed. The effectual fervent prayer of a righteous man availeth much. (James 5:14—16)

But other of the apostles saw I none, save James the Lord's brother. (Galatians 1:19)

Nor of men sought we glory, neither of you, nor yet of others, when we might have been burdensome, as the apostles of Christ. (1 Thessalonians 2:6)

A.D. 50 (Time of 1 Corinthians: 53—55 A.D., 2 Corinthians: 55—56 A.D., and Romans: 57 A.D.)

> And when Paul had laid his hands upon them, the Holy Ghost came on them; and they spake with tongues, and prophesied. (Acts 19:6)

> And God wrought special miracles by the hands of Paul: So that from his body were brought unto the sick handkerchiefs or aprons, and the diseases departed from them, and the evil spirits went out of them. (Acts 19:11—12)

> For I think that God hath set forth us the apostles last, as it were appointed to death: for we are made a spectacle unto the world, and to angels, and to men. (1 Corinthians 4:9)

> Now concerning spiritual gifts, brethren, I would not have you ignorant. Ye know that ye were Gentiles, carried away unto these dumb idols, even as ye were led. Wherefore I give you to understand, that no man speaking by the Spirit of God calleth Jesus accursed: and that no man can say that Jesus is the Lord, but by the Holy Ghost. Now there are diversities of gifts, but the same Spirit. And there are differences of administrations, but the same Lord. And there are diversities of

operations, but it is the same God which worketh all in all.

But the manifestation of the Spirit is given to every man to profit withal. For to one is given by the Spirit the word of wisdom; to another the word of knowledge by the same Spirit; To another faith by the same Spirit; to another the gifts of healing by the same Spirit; To another the working of miracles; to another prophecy; to another discerning of spirits; to another divers kinds of tongues; to another the interpretation of tongues: But all these worketh that one and the selfsame Spirit, dividing to every man severally as he will. For as the body is one, and hath many members, and all the members of that one body, being many, are one body: so also is Christ. For by one Spirit are we all baptized into one body, whether we be Jews or Gentiles, whether we be bond or free; and have been all made to drink into one Spirit. For the body is not one member, but many.

If the foot shall say, Because I am not the hand, I am not of the body; is it therefore not of the body? And if the ear shall say, Because I am not the eye, I am not of the body; is it therefore not of the body? If the whole body were an eye, where were the hearing? If the whole were hearing, where were the smelling? But now hath

Why Cessationism Can't Be True

God set the members every one of them in the body, as it hath pleased him. And if they were all one member, where were the body? But now are they many members, yet but one body. And the eye cannot say unto the hand, I have no need of thee: nor again the head to the feet, I have no need of you.

Nay, much more those members of the body, which seem to be more feeble, are necessary: And those members of the body, which we think to be less honourable, upon these we bestow more abundant honour; and our uncomely parts have more abundant comeliness. For our comely parts have no need: but God hath tempered the body together, having given more abundant honour to that part which lacked: That there should be no schism in the body; but that the members should have the same care one for another. And whether one member suffer, all the members suffer with it; or one member be honoured, all the members rejoice with it.

Now ye are the body of Christ, and members in particular. And God hath set some in the church, first apostles, secondarily prophets, thirdly teachers, after that miracles, then gifts of healings, helps, governments, diversities of tongues. Are all apostles? are all prophets? are all teachers? are all workers of miracles? Have all the gifts of healing? do all speak with tongues? do all interpret? But covet earnestly the best gifts: and yet shew I unto you a more excellent way. (1 Corinthians 12:1—31)

Charity never faileth: but whether there be prophecies, they shall fail; whether there be tongues, they shall cease; whether there be knowledge, it shall vanish away. For we know in part, and we prophesy in part. But when that which is perfect is come, then that which is in part shall be done away. When I was a child, I spake as a child, I understood as a child, I thought as a child: but when I became a man, I put away childish things. For now we see through a glass, darkly; but then face to face: now I know in part; but then shall I know even as also I am known. (1 Corinthians 13:8—12)

Follow after charity, and desire spiritual gifts, but rather that ye may prophesy. For he that speaketh in an unknown tongue speaketh not unto men, but unto God: for no man understandeth him; howbeit in the spirit he speaketh mysteries. But he that prophesieth speaketh unto men to edification, and exhortation, and comfort. He that speaketh in an unknown tongue edifieth himself; but he that prophesieth edifieth the church. I would that ye all spake with tongues, but rather that ye prophesied: for greater is he that prophesieth than he that speaketh with tongues, except he interpret, that the church may receive edifying.

Now, brethren, if I come unto you speaking with tongues, what shall I profit you, except I shall speak to you either by revelation, or by knowledge, or by prophesying, or by doctrine? And even things without life giving sound, whether pipe or harp, except they give a distinction in the sounds, how shall it be known what is piped or harped? For if the trumpet give an uncertain sound, who shall prepare himself to the battle? So likewise ye, except ye utter by the tongue words easy to be understood, how shall it be known what is spoken? for ye shall speak into the air. There are, it may be, so many kinds of voices in the world, and none of them is without signification. Therefore if I know not the meaning of the voice, I shall be unto him that speaketh a barbarian, and he that speaketh shall be a barbarian unto me.

Even so ye, forasmuch as ye are zealous of spiritual gifts, seek that ye may excel to the edifying of the church. Wherefore let him that speaketh in an unknown tongue pray that he may interpret. For if I pray in an unknown tongue, my spirit prayeth, but my understanding is unfruitful. What is it then? I will pray with the spirit, and I will pray with the understanding also: I will sing with the spirit, and I will sing with the understanding also. Else when thou shalt bless with the spirit, how shall he that occupieth the room of the unlearned say Amen at thy giving of thanks, seeing he understandeth not what thou sayest? For thou verily givest thanks well, but the other is not edified.

I thank my God, I speak with tongues more than ye all: Yet in the church I had rather speak five words with my understanding, that by my voice I might teach others also, than ten thousand words in an unknown tongue. Brethren, be not children in understanding: howbeit in malice be ye children, but in understanding be men. In the law it is written, With men of other tongues and other lips will I speak unto this people; and yet for all that will they not hear me, saith the Lord. Wherefore tongues are for a sign, not to them that believe, but to them that believe not: but prophesying serveth not for them that believe not, but for them which believe.

If therefore the whole church be come together into one place, and all speak with tongues, and there come in those that are unlearned, or unbelievers, will they not say that ye are mad? But if all prophesy, and there come in one that believeth not, or one unlearned, he is convinced of all, he is judged of all: And thus are the secrets of his heart made manifest; and so falling down on his face he will worship God, and report that God is in you of a truth. How is it then, brethren? when ye come together, every one of you hath a psalm, hath a doctrine, hath a tongue, hath a revelation, hath an interpretation. Let all things be done unto edifying.

If any man speak in an unknown tongue, let it be by two, or at the most by three, and that by course; and let one interpret. But if there be no interpreter, let him keep silence in the church; and let him speak to himself, and to God. Let the prophets speak two or three, and let the other judge. If any thing be revealed to another that sitteth by, let the first hold his peace. For ye may all prophesy one by one, that all may learn, and all may be comforted. And the spirits of the prophets are subject to the prophets. For God is not the author of confusion, but of peace, as in all churches of the saints.

Let your women keep silence in the churches: for it is not permitted unto them to speak; but they are commanded to be under obedience, as also saith the law. And if they will learn any thing, let them ask their husbands at home: for it is a shame for women to speak in the church. What? came the word of God out from you? or came it unto you only? If any man think himself to be a prophet, or spiritual, let him acknowledge that the things that I write unto you are the commandments of the Lord. But if any man be ignorant, let him be ignorant. Wherefore, brethren, covet to prophesy, and forbid not to speak with tongues. Let all things be done decently and in order. (1 Corinthians 14)

Truly the signs of an apostle were wrought among you in all patience, in signs, and wonders, and mighty deeds. (2 Corinthians 12:12)

Having then gifts differing according to the grace that is given to us, whether prophecy, let us prophesy according to the proportion of faith; Or ministry, let us wait on our ministering: or he that teacheth, on teaching; Or he that exhorteth, on exhortation: he that giveth, let him do it with simplicity; he that ruleth, with diligence; he that sheweth mercy, with cheerfulness. (Romans 12:6—8)

Through mighty signs and wonders, by the power of the Spirit of God; so that from Jerusalem, and round about unto

Illyricum, I have fully preached the gospel of Christ. (Romans 15:19)

Salute Andronicus and Junia, my kinsmen, and my fellowprisoners, who are of note among the apostles, who also were in Christ before me. (Romans 16:7)

And the same man had four daughters, virgins, which did prophesy. And as we tarried there many days, there came down from Judaea a certain prophet, named Agabus. (Acts 21:9—10)

A.D. 60 (During Paul's journey to Rome, time of Ephesians: 62 A.D. and Hebrews: 65 A.D.)

And it came to pass, that the father of Publius lay sick of a fever and of a bloody flux: to whom Paul entered in, and prayed, and laid his hands on him, and healed him. So when this was done, others also, which had diseases in the island, came, and were healed. (Acts 28:8—9)

Wherefore he saith, When he ascended up on high, he led captivity captive, and gave gifts unto men. (Now that he ascended, what is it but that he also descended first into the lower parts of the earth? He that descended is the same also that ascended up far above all heavens, that he might fill all things.)

> And he gave some, apostles; and some, prophets; and some, evangelists; and some, pastors and teachers; For the perfecting of the saints, for the work of the ministry, for the edifying of the body of Christ: Till we all come in the unity of the faith, and of the knowledge of the Son of God, unto a perfect man, unto the measure of the stature of the fulness of Christ. (Ephesians 4:8—13)

> Neglect not the gift that is in thee, which was given thee by prophecy, with the laying on of the hands of the presbytery. (1 Timothy 4:14)

> That ye may be mindful of the words which were spoken before by the holy prophets, and of the commandment of us the apostles of the Lord and Saviour. (2 Peter 3:2)

A.D. 90

And he said unto me, Thou must prophesy again before many peoples, and nations, and tongues, and kings. (Revelation 10:11)

Notice that there were still sign gifts being performed, even in the last epistle written. From A.D. 30 to A.D. 95, there were still sign gifts being used. Thus, we can conclude that there is no evidence of sign gifts ceasing according to the occurrence of it in the New Testament. There was no transition between

Why Cessationism Can't Be True

1 Corinthians and 2 Corinthians. Prophecy did not end, as Cessationists like to use Hebrews 1:1—3 to support that view. John continued to prophesy even 20 years after the Book of Hebrews was written. If Christ came to replace the prophets, why was John still prophesying even after Christ had risen, and even after he finished the writing of Revelation?

6

Apostles

The issue that makes Cessationists so adamant about accepting the continuation of apostles is their misperception of who apostles are and what their role in the Church is. They usually view apostles as specially-empowered ambassadors who were foundational to the Church and have witnessed the resurrection of Christ and had inspired authority worthy of writing Scripture. But that is not necessarily who they are. Let's look closer at this gift, and clear up the misunderstandings involved.

What is an apostle?

The Greek word for "apostle" (*apostolos*) means "delegate, ambassador, commissioner, or messenger." An apostle is someone delegated by Christ to be an ambassador for Him and a commissioner of the Gospel and a messenger of the truth. They are what most today would call "missionaries."

What is the purpose of apostles?

As is observed throughout the book of Acts, apostles were sent out to establish churches. They were responsible for going into regions and places where the Gospel had not yet been given. They introduce the Gospel into a region and establish churches. They then appoint pastors to lead the churches and evangelists to continue giving the Gospel while they themselves go to another region to introduce the Gospel.

From Paul, we learn that apostles are "foundation layers." In 1 Corinthians 3:10—11, Paul says,

> According to the grace of God which is given unto me, as a wise masterbuilder, I have laid the foundation, and another buildeth thereon. But let every man take heed how he buildeth thereupon. For other foundation can no man lay than that is laid, which is Jesus Christ.

In Romans 15:20, he says,

> Yea, so have I strived to preach the gospel, not where Christ was named, lest I should build upon another man's foundation.

Apostles lay the foundation of Christ and the Gospel in new (or foreign) regions for others to build upon.

What does an apostle do?

1) *An apostle preaches the Gospel to new regions.*

Yea, so have I strived to preach the gospel, not where Christ was named, lest I should build upon another man's foundation. (Romans 15:20)

2) *An apostle plants churches and ordains pastors and evangelists to continue the ministry in the churches.*

For this cause left I thee in Crete, that thou shouldest set in order the things that are wanting, and ordain elders in every city, as I had appointed thee. (Titus 1:5) And when they had ordained them elders in every church, and had prayed with fasting, they commended them to the Lord, on whom they believed. (Acts 14:23)

3) *An apostle disciples new converts, usually until a pastor takes his place.*

And he continued there a year and six months, teaching the word of God among them. (Acts 18:11)

4) *An apostle checks up on the churches he established, and mentors its pastors.*

And in this confidence I was minded to come unto you before, that ye might have a second benefit; And to pass by you into Macedonia, and to come again out of Macedonia unto you, and of you to be brought on my way toward Judaea. (2 Corinthians 1:15—16)

For this cause have I sent unto you Timotheus, who is my beloved son, and faithful in the Lord, who shall bring you into remembrance of my ways which be in Christ, as I teach every where in every church. Now some are puffed up, as though I would not come to you. But I will come to you shortly, if the Lord will, and will know, not the speech of them which are puffed up, but the power. For the kingdom of God is not in word, but in power. What will ye? shall I come unto you with a rod, or in love, and in the spirit of meekness? (1 Corinthians 4:17—21)

And if any man hunger, let him eat at home; that ye come not together unto condemnation. And the rest will I set in order when I come. (1 Corinthians 11:34)

Do all apostles write Scripture?

No. Not even all the 12 Apostles wrote Scripture, including Philipp, Bartholomew, Andrew, Matthias, and Simon.

Were there only 12 apostles plus Paul?

No. There were more apostles besides the 12 and Paul. Barnabas (Acts 14:4, 14), Silvanus (1 Thessalonians 1:1, 2:6), and Timotheus (1 Thessalonians 1:1, 2:6) were also apostles, and probably even Andronicus and Junia (Romans 16:7). There was also the 70 mentioned in Luke 10. Notice also in 1 Corinthians 15:5—8, that Christ was seen of the 12 Apostles, and then later He was seen "of all the apostles" (there were not just 12), and then after that, He was seen of Paul.

Are apostles infallible and inerrant?

No. Clearly there were questions that the apostles debated on (see Acts 15), and there were strifes among them (see Galatians 2:11—14 and Acts 15:39). The apostles were just as human as we are, and their doctrine was not inerrant except when they were inspired as they wrote Scripture.

How much authority do apostles have?

Certainly the 12 Apostles had more authority than apostles after them because they have actually been with Christ and witnessed His resurrection. The new converts then had no choice but to believe the doctrine they taught. But God used certain of them specifically to write Scripture (our New Testament) so that those after will have inerrant doctrine provided for them. Again, not all the apostles wrote Scripture, just those that were inspired to write Scripture. The authority of Scripture has nothing to do with apostleship. God used apostles just like he used kings to write Scripture. Being an apostle does not mean you can write Scripture or have unquestioned authority. Not even the early apostles had the right to pope-like authority (2 Corinthians 1:24).

Apostles have some level of authority over their churches because those that were converted under their ministry have somewhat no choice but to adhere to them, because the apostles are more mature in their faith and were the ones that led them to Christianity. Their authority is more a kind of respect, because apostles are generally more knowledgeable and mature. Their authority also comes, not from themselves, but from their office. They have as much authority as elders/bishops. That authority is mainly for the purpose of unity and efficient church operation. And be aware that this is not authority for truth or practice. Throughout Acts 15, apostles and elders are seen as co-existent, collaborating with each other. The elders did not have to be subject to the apostles, but had the same level of authority as they.

As far as authority for truth goes, apostles use the same authority as the rest of believers—the Scriptures. Notice in Acts that the apostles preached out of the Old Testament. They did not just say that Christ was the Messiah based on what they witnessed, but based on the prophecies of the Old Testament. When they preached, the Holy Spirit commended what they were saying in the hearts of the hearers (Acts 14:3, 1 Corinthians 3:6—7). Except when they were inspired to write Scripture, the early apostles did not have any kind of personal authority for truth. Their accuracy in truth was not so much because of them, but because of the Holy Spirit within them, who guided them into all truth and brought to remembrance whatsoever Christ had taught them (John 14:26, 16:13).

Apostolic Authority

There is a different kind of authority, however, that I want to explain—apostolic authority. Luke 9:1-2 says,

> Then he (Jesus) called his twelve disciples together, and gave them power and authority over all devils, and to cure diseases. And he sent them to preach the kingdom of God, and to heal the sick.

Paul said that he could boast of his authority as an apostle of Christ (2 Corinthians 10:8). What is apostolic authority? I think it would help to recall the definition of "apostle." An apostle is a messenger. Therefore consider the authority that a messenger has when he proclaims the message of the king to the people. It's not that the messenger is one who has authority, but that he is bearing the authority of the king. He is not speaking for himself, but for the king. His commands are not from himself, but from the king. It is also the kind of authority that a master gives to the stewards of his household. It is not that the steward has authority in or of himself, but that he bears the authority of the master. He is responsible for making sure the house is functioning as the master would like it.

> For the Son of man is as a man taking a far journey, who left his house, and gave authority to his servants, and to every man his work, and commanded the porter to watch. (Mark 13:34)

Now consider that in relation to the messengers/servants of God.

> Let a man so account of us, as of the ministers of Christ, and stewards of the mysteries of God (1 Corinthians 4:1)

> And Jesus came and said to them, "All authority in heaven and on earth has been given to me. Go therefore... (Matthew 28:18-19, ESV)

Any messenger of God has "apostolic authority" because he is bearing the authoritative message of God. Yes, the apostles in the Scriptures had authority, but that authority was only because they were speaking the words of God. Apostles today have that authority because they are speaking the words of God recorded in the Scriptures.

What about Acts 1:21—26?

> Wherefore of these men which have companied with us all the time that the Lord Jesus went in and out among us,

> Beginning from the baptism of John, unto that same day that he was taken up from us, must one be ordained to be a witness with us of his resurrection. And they appointed two, Joseph called Barsabas, who was surnamed Justus, and Matthias. And they prayed, and said, Thou, Lord, which knowest the hearts of all men, shew whether of these two thou hast chosen, That he may take part of this ministry and apostleship, from which Judas by transgression fell, that he might go to his own place. And they gave forth their lots; and the lot fell upon Matthias; and he was numbered with the eleven apostles.

Cessationists use this passage to say that a requirement to be an apostle included being an eyewitness of the resurrection of Christ. Notice in verse 22, however, that they did not mention that they needed one who was also a witness of the resurrection to be an *apostle*, but rather *one of the twelve* (v. 26). They were looking for someone who would "take part of *this* ministry and apostleship, from which Judas by transgression fell, that he might go to his own place" (v. 25).

What about 1 Corinthians 15:8—9?

> And last of all he was seen of me also, as of one born out of due time. For I am the least of the apostles, that am not meet to be called an apostle, because I persecuted the church of God.

Cessationists also use this passage to say that being an eye-witness of the resurrection of Christ was a requirement for apostleship. Notice, however, that in verse 8, Paul is not saying that he was an apostle as of one born out of due time, but that he witnessed the resurrected Christ as of one born out of due time. Also, in verse 9, Paul is not the least of the apostles because he was "the last of them," but because he persecuted the Church of God, as noted in the verse.

What about Ephesians 2:20?

> And are built upon the foundation of the apostles and prophets, Jesus Christ himself being the chief corner stone.

Cessationists assume that the apostles and prophets are the foundation of the Church, with Christ as the chief cornerstone. They then argue that since apostles are foundational, they cannot continue to be given because we have moved on to the building itself, and a foundation cannot continue to be laid. The main problem with this, however, is that the foundation is not the apostles themselves. Christ is the foundation; the apostles are the ones who lay the foundation.

When we read, "The Epistle of Paul," we do not conclude that Paul is the epistle; rather, we conclude that Paul wrote the epistle. When we read, "the foundations of the wall" (Revelation 21:19), we do not conclude that the wall is the foundation. When we hear, "the foundation of the house," we do not conclude that the house is the foundation; we conclude that house is built on and supported by the foundation. In

Why Cessationism Can't Be True

the same way, when we read, "the foundation of the apostles," we do not conclude that the apostles are the foundation; rather, we conclude that the apostles laid the foundation and are supported by and built on the foundation like we are. This perspective is not heretical like the previous, "for other foundation can no man lay than that is laid, which is Jesus Christ" (1 Corinthians 3:11).

Then why does Paul say that Christ is the chief cornerstone, and not the foundation? Well, the apostles and prophets' message included many teachings, but the central theme (the chief cornerstone) of their message was Christ. The cornerstone is the foundation, as we see in Isaiah 28:16, which says,

> Therefore thus saith the Lord GOD, Behold, I lay in Zion for a foundation a stone, a tried stone, a precious corner stone, a sure foundation: he that believeth shall not make haste.

The apostles and prophets lay the foundation, which is the Gospel. The chief cornerstone of that foundation is Jesus Christ.

Still Continuing

According to Ephesians 4:11—13, apostleship does not end until Christ comes back. It says,

> And he gave some, apostles; and some, prophets; and some, evangelists; and some, pastors and teachers; For the perfecting of

> the saints, for the work of the ministry, for the edifying of the body of Christ: Till we all come in the unity of the faith, and of the knowledge of the Son of God, unto a perfect man, unto the measure of the stature of the fulness of Christ.

He gave apostles and the other offices to the Church until we are all unified (and we're not yet, seeing there are still denominations and splits in the Church), until we become fully mature (which has definitely not happened yet), and until we measure up to Christ's stature (which also clearly hasn't happened yet). All those characteristics of when apostleship and the other offices will end clearly portray the end of time when Christ returns to gather His Church.

You have to be consistent with the text. If apostleship doesn't apply to the fulfillment of this passage, neither do the other offices. Don't add any of your own assertions into the text. It says what it says. All of those offices, including apostleship, are given until the Day of the Lord.

> Therefore also said the wisdom of God, I will send them prophets and apostles, and some of them they shall slay and persecute (Luke 11:49)

7
Prophets and Prophecy

The chief reason why some people believe that there are no more prophets in the Church is due to the misunderstandings about what a prophet is and the purpose of prophets in the Church. They perceive prophets as infallible, authoritative messengers of God that foretell future events and establish Scripture. Some of that is true, but some is not. Prophets were not infallible, and they were not authoritative—though they were messengers of God. Sometimes they foretell future events, and only certain of the prophets have written Scripture, which was under the inspiration of God. Permit me to explain more, using Scripture.

What is a prophet?

The word "prophecy" comes from the Greek word "*propheteia*," which means "prediction." The word "prophet" comes from the Greek word "*prophetes*" which means "foreteller; one who speaks under inspiration." A prophet is one who foretells future events and speaks under the inspiration received from God. The gift of prophecy is being able to predict future happenings through the revelation of the Holy Spirit. For example, Agabus was a New Testament prophet who foretold that Paul would be arrested in Jerusalem (Acts 21:10—11), and what he said was fulfilled as soon as Paul went there.

What is the purpose of a prophet?

God uses prophets to communicate His message to mankind.

> I have also spoken by the prophets, and I have multiplied visions, and used similitudes, by the ministry of the prophets. (Hosea 12:10)

> And the LORD spake by his servants the prophets, saying. (2 Kings 21:10)

Prophets express God's thoughts and impending judgment toward churches, and exhort believers and leaders through prophecy and revelation of God's will. They, such like John Knox, are used by God to reform churches and warn the wicked generations and backsliding Christians of God's judgment—not just to prophesy. They are God's reformers. According to Ephesians 4:11—12, prophets are given "for the perfecting of the saints, for the work of the ministry, for the edifying of the body of Christ."

Apostles are primary in the Church, and prophets follow in second (1 Corinthians 12:28). The orders are not of importance or rank necessarily, but of sequence

Why Cessationism Can't Be True

in the building and establishing of the local churches. Why are prophets second? According to Ephesians 2:20, prophets take part in laying the foundation (which is Christ and the Gospel) for the Church. They work with apostles to plant the seed of the Gospel and provide the spark for Christianity in heathen nations. They are greatly used by God to present His vision and His will to the apostles.

What does a prophet do?

1) *A prophet foretells future events, minor or major, by the revelation of the Spirit.*
   And in these days came prophets from Jerusalem unto Antioch. And there stood up one of them named Agabus, and signified by the Spirit that there should be great dearth throughout all the world: which came to pass in the days of Claudius Caesar. (Acts 11:27—28)

2) *A prophet warns people of impending judgment or against doing something, through the burdening of the Spirit.*
   Yet he sent prophets to them, to bring them again unto the LORD; and they testified against them: but they would not give ear. (2 Chronicles 24:19)
   Yet the LORD testified against Israel, and against Judah, by all the prophets, and by all the seers, saying, Turn ye from your evil ways, and keep my commandments and my statutes, according to all the law which I commanded your fathers, and which I sent to you by my servants the prophets. (2 Kings 17:13)
   And the LORD spake by his servants the prophets, saying, Because Manasseh king of Judah hath done these abominations, and hath done wickedly above all that the Amorites did, which were before him, and hath made Judah also to sin with his idols: Therefore thus saith the LORD God of Israel, Behold, I am

bringing such evil upon Jerusalem and Judah, that whosoever heareth of it, both his ears shall tingle. And I will stretch over Jerusalem the line of Samaria, and the plummet of the house of Ahab: and I will wipe Jerusalem as a man wipeth a dish, wiping it, and turning it upside down. (2 Kings 21:10—13)

3) *A prophet communicates God's will for a nation, church, or individual through the revelation of the Spirit.*
Now there were in the church that was at Antioch certain prophets and teachers; as Barnabas, and Simeon that was called Niger, and Lucius of Cyrene, and Manaen, which had been brought up with Herod the tetrarch, and Saul. As they ministered to the Lord, and fasted, the Holy Ghost said, Separate me Barnabas and Saul for the work whereunto I have called them. And when they had fasted and prayed, and laid their hands on them, they sent them away. (Acts 13:1—3)

4) *A prophet exhorts and strengthens other believers.*
And Judas and Silas, being prophets also themselves, exhorted the brethren with many words, and confirmed them. (Acts 15:42)
But he that prophesieth speaketh unto men to edification, and exhortation, and comfort. (1 Corinthians 14:3)

5) *A prophet exposes the secrets of the heart under the revelation of the Spirit.*
But if all prophesy, and there come in one that believeth not, or one unlearned, he is convinced of all, he is judged of all: And thus are the secrets of his heart made manifest; and so falling down on his face he will worship God, and report that God is in you of a truth. (1 Corinthians 14:24—25)

Do all prophets write Scripture?

No. There were undoubtedly prophets in the Corinthian church (1 Corinthians 12, 14), and we don't have any of their prophecies in Scripture. Philipp's four daughters prophesied (Acts 21:8—9), but we don't have any of their prophecies written in Scripture either.

What is the prophet's authority for truth?

God's Word, along with the commendation/confirmation from the Holy Spirit in the heart, has always been the authority for truth, even for prophets. The Spirit uses the Word of God as its sword/tool/instrument.

> So shall my word be that goeth forth out of my mouth: it shall not return unto me void, but it shall accomplish that which I please, and it shall prosper in the thing whereto I sent it. (Isaiah 55:11)

When one speaks the words of God, the Spirit uses it to pierce and transform hearts. When one speaks the words of God, the Spirit confirms the message to the hearers. We all have this privilege and opportunity, for we have the Scriptures.

But God still speaks to His Church, not only through a record of universal truths, but also through His prophets with private messages relevant to it. The Book is not authoritative, but the words of God contained in it are. The prophet is not authoritative, but the words of God he speaks are.

How do you know that what a prophet is speaking are indeed the words of God? Just as you would know that the Bible is the Word of God—by the commendation of the Spirit in the heart. How would you validate whether or not one who claimed to be a prophet was in fact speaking for God? Just as those in the Old Testament would—by observing the fulfillment of their prophecies (Deuteronomy 18:21—22). Also, if their message is against God or the Scriptures, even if their prophecy comes to pass, he is a false prophet (Deuteronomy 13:1—3).

Doesn't the completion of Scripture mean that there will be no more divine revelations and, thus, no more prophets?

No. God is not one who just writes a book for us to read and then watches us live it out. He is a personal God that continues to speak to His children. Why pray and listen to God if He doesn't speak to us? How do you know what God's will is for your life if He doesn't reveal it to you? If God can reveal things to you, then He can certainly do the same with prophets. Just because prophets wrote the Scriptures, that doesn't mean they ceased when the Scriptures were completed. These prophets were saints and disciples as well—does that mean saints and disciples ceased to exist because the Scriptures were completed? Not at all! God used prophets to write the Scriptures, but that was not His only purpose for prophets. He used many kinds of people to make the Scriptures under His inspiration: princes, kings, shepherds, psalmists, judges, prophets, apostles, and Christ Himself. Did any of these vocations cease just because certain people with that vocation wrote the Scriptures? Of course not!

What about *Sola Scriptura*?

One of the key principles of Protestantism that separates itself from Catholicism is *Sola Scriptura*. This is Latin for "Scripture Alone." Since this is a principle we very much agree with, doesn't that mean that we must reject any extra-biblical revelation? No, it does not. Permit me to explain.

Sola Scriptura does not mean that the Scriptures are our only source of information. We can communicate with others outside of using the Scriptures. We can learn extra-biblical things outside of is as well. Then what does *Sola Scriptura* mean? It means that all the dogmas of our faith must be based on Scripture alone. Second Timothy 2:15—16 says,

> And that from a child thou hast known the holy scriptures, which are able to make thee wise unto salvation through faith which is in Christ Jesus. All scripture is given by inspiration of God, and is profitable for doctrine, for reproof, for correction, for instruction in righteousness.

Salvation, doctrine, reproof, correction, and instruction in righteousness must be grounded in the written Word of God. There is no new revelation on salvation, or on doctrine, or on reproof, or on correction, or on instruction in righteousness. However, that does not mean there are no more revelations from God at all. God still reveals things to us outside of salvation and doctrine. Look back at what a prophet does. None of those functions of a prophet interfere with the dogmas of the Church provided by Scripture. What God may reveal to someone is not a doctrinal truth, but a special message to an individual, a local church, a movement, or a nation. While the Scriptures communicate universal truths, prophets give specific messages that are unqualified to be written in Scripture. God still speaks, for He is a personal God who communicates with His children.

What about false prophets?

Keep in mind, there are false prophets. Not everyone out there who claims to be a prophet is a prophet of God.

> I have not sent these prophets, yet they ran: I have not spoken to them, yet they prophesied.... I have heard what the prophets said, that prophesy lies in my name, saying, I have dreamed, I have dreamed. How long shall this be in the heart of the prophets that prophesy lies? yea, they are prophets of the deceit of their own heart. (Jeremiah 23:21, 25—26)

Many Cessationists point to these false prophets, and say, "See! Modern prophets are counterfeit, unbiblical liars! There are no prophets anymore!" But those are the false prophets that they find fault with. What about the true prophets like George Wishart and John Knox? Just because there are false prophets doesn't mean there are no true prophets. There are false teachers, but that does not mean there are no true teachers.

Does a false prophecy make one a false prophet?

No. Though every word of God is true, prophets are still capable of misunderstanding or misapplying His message. Efficiency in prophecy requires growth and time, just as with any other leadership ministry. A false prophecy does not mean one is a false prophet; it merely means he is human. The same could be applied to teaching. Teachers can unintentionally teach error, but that does not make them false teachers. That is why everything must be tested against the Scriptures. Now notice that I said that they may "unintentionally" teach or prophesy something falsely. If a person taught or prophesied falsely intentionally, then that means they are false teachers or prophets, and should be avoided.

In 1 Corinthians 14:29, Paul says, "Let the prophets speak two or three, and let the other judge." Why would others need to judge (i.e. evaluate) the prophet's message if it was inevitable that a true prophet would prophesy accurately every time? In 1 Thessalonians 5:20, Paul says, "Despise not prophesyings." It's seems quite clear from this verse that there were people that did not like prophecies. Why would they despise such messages from God? Because prophets would get the message wrong sometimes or many times, and it annoyed people. First Corinthians 13:9 says, "For we know in part, and we prophesy in part."

How do we judge a prophet's message?

1) *Compare it with God's truth in the Scriptures.*
   If there arise among you a prophet, or a dreamer of dreams, and giveth thee a sign or a wonder, And the sign or the wonder come to pass, whereof he spake unto thee, saying, Let us go after other gods, which thou hast not known, and let us serve them; Thou shalt not hearken unto the words of that prophet, or that dreamer of dreams: for the LORD your God proveth you, to know whether ye love the LORD your God with all your heart and with all your soul. (Deuteronomy 13:1—3)

2) *Examine whether he believes the fundamental doctrines of the faith.*
   Beloved, believe not every spirit, but try the spirits whether they are of God: because many false prophets are gone out into the world. Hereby know ye the Spirit of God: Every spirit that confesseth that Jesus Christ is come in the flesh is of God: And every spirit that confesseth not that Jesus Christ is come in the flesh is not of God: and this is that spirit of antichrist, whereof ye have heard that it should come; and even now already is it in the world. (1 John 4:1—3)

3) *Seek approval from the Holy Spirit.*
   We are of God: he that knoweth God heareth us; he that is not of God heareth not us. Hereby know we the spirit of truth, and the spirit of error. (1 John 4:6)

4) *Examine his fruit.*
   Beware of false prophets, which come to you in sheep's clothing, but inwardly they are ravening wolves. Ye shall know them by their fruits. Do men gather grapes of thorns, or figs of thistles? Even so every good tree bringeth forth good fruit; but a corrupt tree bringeth forth evil fruit. A good tree cannot bring forth evil fruit, neither can a corrupt tree bring forth good fruit. Every tree that bringeth not forth good fruit is hewn

down, and cast into the fire. Wherefore by their fruits ye shall know them. (Matthew 7:15—20)

5) *Seek the counsel of other prophets and those with the gift of discerning between spirits.*
Let the prophets speak two or three, and let the other judge. (1 Corinthians 14:29)
To another the working of miracles; to another prophecy; to another discerning of spirits; to another divers kinds of tongues; to another the interpretation of tongues. (1 Corinthians 12:10)
The Body takes care of itself. God has given certain gifts to certain members in the Body so that there will be unity, balance, and interdependency. God is aware that it can be difficult to discern whether a prophet is speaking truth or not, so that is why He gives some in the Body the gift of discerning between spirits. Just like there are certain members in our physical body that keep each other in check, the gifts given to the members of Christ's Body are there to keep each other in check.

What about Hebrews 1:1—2?

> God, who at sundry times and in divers manners spake in time past unto the fathers by the prophets, Hath in these last days spoken unto us by his Son, whom he hath appointed heir of all things, by whom also he made the worlds.

To some, this passage may seem to imply that God doesn't speak through prophets anymore; however, this passage is merely saying that God sent His Son to speak to us. It is emphasizing our higher privilege to have God's Son speaking to us. It is not in any way nullifying the office of a prophet. If Christ came to replace the prophets, why were there still prophets being added even after Christ had ascended into heaven, and after the four Gospels were written?

Also consider the words "last days." If these are the last days, then what was said in Acts 2:17—18 is true for today.

> And it shall come to pass in the last days, saith God, I will pour out of my Spirit upon all flesh: and your sons and your daughters shall prophesy, and your young men shall see visions, and your old men shall dream dreams: And on my servants and on my handmaidens I will pour out in those days of my Spirit; and they shall prophesy.

What about 2 Peter 1:19?

> We have also a more sure word of prophecy; whereunto ye do well that ye take heed, as unto a light that shineth in a dark place, until the day dawn, and the day star arise in your hearts.

Some might say we don't need prophets anymore, because we have a more sure word of prophecy (the Bible). Prophets can turn out to be false, but the Scriptures are perfect and true. The problem, however, is that there were still prophecies even after this was written (the book of Revelation, for example). But regardless, the Scriptures are surer than a prophet's words, but that does not mean we exclude the prophet's words.

What about Jude 1:3?

> Beloved, when I gave all diligence to write unto you of the common salvation, it was needful for me to write unto you, and exhort you that ye should earnestly contend for the faith which was once delivered unto the saints.

Cessationists emphasize the phrase at the end, "the faith which was once delivered unto the saints." They stress the word "once" to say that revelation was given to the Church once and is not to be given anymore. But this is talking about the faith, not revelation—"the faith" being Christianity.

What about Revelation 22:18?

> For I testify unto every man that heareth the words of the prophecy of this book, If any man shall add unto these things, God shall add unto him the plagues that are written in this book.

This is last book of the Bible written, and John warns everyone to not add to the prophecies in it. Doesn't that mean we cannot prophesy? Not at all! It means that we can't add any prophecies to the Scriptures (or more specifically, the book of Revelation). There are false prophets, and they may end up adding their false prophecies to Scripture, and that would make the Bible very confusing and deterring. Simply put, the passage is advocating the closed cannon of Scripture or the book of Revelation itself.

What about Daniel 9:24?

> Seventy weeks are determined upon thy people and upon thy holy city, to finish the transgression, and to make an end of sins, and to make reconciliation for iniquity, and to bring in everlasting righteousness, and to seal up the vision and prophecy, and to anoint the most Holy.

Some Cessationists say that this verse (and the verses after it) refers to the year 70 A.D. when the Jerusalem temple was destroyed. Because of this view, they can then conclude that vision and prophecy was sealed up (in their minds "ended") when the temple was destroyed, which was also around the time of the completion of the New Testament.

However, there are so many variables in the prophecy. Are the "70 weeks" a literal period of 70 weeks, or is it figurative? Has this prophecy already happened, or will it unfold in the future? After all, has transgression finished? Has sin ceased? Has everlasting righteousness been established?

Also, what is meant by the statement "to seal up the prophecy and vision"? The word "to seal up" could imply "to end," "to conclude," or it could be actually be figurative of a seal. And for some, "sealing up" connotes the idea of "closing," as to a final end. But "sealing up" could also have the idea of "making permanent," or "securing in place," as is the case in

Ephesians 1:13 (being sealed with the Holy Spirit). This interpretation seems to be more congruent with bringing in everlasting righteousness, which was also stated in Daniel 9:24. Another thing to consider is that "sealing" is a sign of authentication, as we see with the kings of those days. The sealing of the prophecy and vision may not mean an ending of the prophecy and vision. What's more, is this a specific prophecy and vision, or prophecy and visions in general? But, considering other Scriptures that are more explicit, prophecies and visions will not end until the Day of the Lord, so this passage cannot be suggesting and end to prophecies and visions after the destruction of the Jerusalem temple in 70 A.D.

What about Acts 2:17—21?

> And it shall come to pass in the last days, saith God, I will pour out of my Spirit upon all flesh: and your sons and your daughters shall prophesy, and your young men shall see visions, and your old men shall dream dreams: And on my servants and on my handmaidens I will pour out in those days of my Spirit; and they shall prophesy: And I will shew wonders in heaven above, and signs in the earth beneath; blood, and fire, and vapour of smoke: The sun shall be turned into darkness, and the moon into blood, before that great and notable day of the Lord come: And it shall come to pass, that whosoever shall call on the name of the Lord shall be saved.

Some Cessationists view this passage as a timeline, in which the beginning is defined by visions and prophesying, the transition is defined by the blood, fire, and smoke (which they believe refers to the destruction of the Jerusalem temple in 70 A.D., the Abomination of Desolation spoken of by the prophet Daniel and Christ), and the latter end is defined by the Gospel. They believe that the visions and prophesying would end once the "Abomination of Desolation" takes place (which has). There are a couple of problems with that reasoning, however.

The first problem is that the blood, fire, and vapor of smoke are not referring to the "Abomination of Desolation." It is referring to what has been happening even as we speak. War, disaster, and destruction. This has been happening even before A.D. 70. Compare it with Matthew 24:6-14:

> And ye shall hear of wars and rumours of wars: see that ye be not troubled: for all these things must come to pass, but the end is not yet. For nation shall rise against nation, and kingdom against kingdom: and there shall be famines, and pestilences, and earthquakes, in divers places. All these are the beginning of sorrows. Then shall they deliver you up to be afflicted, and shall kill you: and ye shall be hated of all nations for my name's sake. And then shall many be offended, and shall betray one another, and shall hate one another. And many false prophets shall rise, and shall deceive many. And because iniquity shall

abound, the love of many shall wax cold. But he that shall endure unto the end, the same shall be saved. And this gospel of the kingdom shall be preached in all the world for a witness unto all nations; and then shall the end come.

These are signs that the end is near. So if Acts 2:17—21 is a timeline, the visions and prophesying will not end until the Second Coming of Christ. And whether or not it's a timeline, the prophecy said that their sons and daughters will prophesy, which means it will not be for only one generation, but for generations to come. But if it was a timeline, wouldn't that mean that salvation was only available after the destruction of the temple in 70 A.D. (take another look at the passage)?

A Recent Myth

There has been a myth going around (and certainly the saying is true that if something is stated loud enough and often enough, people will come to believe it) that prophesying not only means "foretelling" but also "forth-telling." Basically, Cessationists tend to teach that the word "prophecy" can also be used for preaching. But where did they come up with that idea?! They claim they got it from the Greek, but that's a lie.

"Propheteuo" means "to foretell." If anything, it is with the implication of "forth-telling." It does not also mean to forth-tell (proclaim; preach); it is only giving the implication of telling forth the prophecy, as opposed to revelation that is not exposed to others. There is "prophecy," and there is "revelation." "Revelation" has to do with internal knowledge; "prophecy" has to do with the communication of the revelation to another individual or group. That is why the Greek word implies "forth-telling" the future, and not just knowing it. There is a different Greek word that is used for "preaching" (*kerugma*). Otherwise, how can one know whether a passage is referring to prophecy or preaching? Now, yes, a "prophet" is one who forth-tells as well as foretells, but "prophecy" and "prophesying" only refer to foretelling.

Still Continuing

According to Ephesians 4:11—13, prophets do not cease until Christ comes back. It says,

> And he gave some, apostles; and some, prophets; and some, evangelists; and some, pastors and teachers; For the perfecting of the saints, for the work of the ministry, for the edifying of the body of Christ: Till we all come in the unity of the faith, and of the knowledge of the Son of God, unto a perfect man, unto the measure of the stature of the fulness of Christ.

He gave prophets and the other offices to the Church until we are all unified (and we're not yet, seeing there are still denominations and splits in the Church), until we become fully mature (which has definitely not happened yet), and until we measure up to Christ's stature (which also clearly hasn't happened

Why Cessationism Can't Be True

yet). All those characteristics of when prophets and the other offices will end clearly portray the end of time when Christ returns to gather His Church. If prophets ended with the completion of Scripture, then you would have to conclude that apostles, pastors, teachers, and evangelists ended as well.

Another passage that signifies when prophecy will end is Acts 2:16—21 (which refers to Joel 2:28—32). It says,

> But this is that which was spoken by the prophet Joel; And it shall come to pass in the last days, saith God, I will pour out of my Spirit upon all flesh: and your sons and your daughters shall prophesy, and your young men shall see visions, and your old men shall dream dreams: And on my servants and on my handmaidens I will pour out in those days of my Spirit; and they shall prophesy: And I will shew wonders in heaven above, and signs in the earth beneath; blood, and fire, and vapor of smoke: The sun shall be turned into darkness, and the moon into blood, before that great and notable day of the Lord come: And it shall come to pass, that whosoever shall call on the name of the Lord shall be saved.

First of all, Peter affirms in verse 17 that the days they were in were the last days and that the prophecy in Joel 2:28—32 have been fulfilled.

Now let's look at that prophecy. God's Spirit will pour out on all flesh, not just kings and prophets as in the Old

Testament. The Spirit has not ceased to be poured out, so the following must still be true. The following includes visions, dreams, and prophecy that will be given to sons and daughters, young men and old men, servants and handmaidens. He will pour out His Spirit upon all flesh in those last days, and they will prophesy. Peter then clarifies at the end of his sermon that the promise of the Spirit is for those whom the Lord called to salvation.

> For the promise is to you and to your children, and to all those afar off, as many as the Lord our God shall call. (Acts 2:39)

During those days spoken of, whoever will call upon the name of the Lord will be saved. In this passage, we see that there were signs signifying the era when the Spirit is poured on all who call upon the Lord's name, and there will be signs signifying the day of the Lord. If they were for the last days (and they were), and we are still in the last days, then prophecy, visions, and dreams are still for these days.

> Now there are diversities of gifts, but the same Spirit. And there are differences of administrations, but the same Lord. And there are diversities of operations, but it is the same God which worketh all in all. But the manifestation of the Spirit is given to every man to profit withal. For to one is given by the Spirit... prophecy... But all these worketh that one and the selfsame Spirit, dividing to every man severally as he will. (1 Corinthians 12:4—11)

And the eye cannot say unto the hand, I have no need of thee: nor again the head to the feet, I have no need of you. (1 Corinthians 12:21)

Follow after charity, and desire spiritual gifts, but rather that ye may prophesy. (1 Corinthians 14:1)

I would that ye all spake with tongues, but rather that ye prophesied: for greater is he that prophesieth than he that speaketh with tongues, except he interpret, that the church may receive edifying. (1 Corinthians 14:5)

...But prophesying serveth not for them that believe not, but for them which believe. (1 Corinthians 14:22b)

For ye may all prophesy one by one, that all may learn, and all may be comforted. (1 Corinthians 14:31)

If any man think himself to be a prophet, or spiritual, let him acknowledge that the things that I write unto you are the commandments of the Lord. But if any man be ignorant, let him be ignorant. Wherefore, brethren, covet to prophesy, and forbid not to speak with tongues. (1 Corinthians 14:37—39)

Having then gifts differing according to the grace that is given to us, whether prophecy, let us prophesy according to the proportion of faith. (Romans 12:6)

Despise not prophesyings. (1 Thessalonians 5:20)

Wherefore, behold, I send unto you prophets, and wise men, and scribes: and some of them ye shall kill and crucify; and some of them shall ye scourge in your synagogues, and persecute them from city to city. (Matthew 23:24)

8

Tongues

The gift of tongues is probably the most attacked by Cessationists because of its bad reputation of being chaotic and hysteric. But we know that its abuse has been true even during the early times of the Church. It was actually common that a whole group of new converts would speak in tongues, just as we see sometimes today. And just because it *was* common does not mean that the gift ceased. It just means that the gift is not as common anymore. Or, maybe the gift of tongues is common, but you just haven't been exposed to much of it.

What is the gift of tongues?

Let's start with the Greek. The Greek word for "tongues" (*glossa*—from which we get the word "glossary") means "tongue; language." The gift of tongues is the ability to communicate in another language.

Nathan J. Page

What is the function and purpose of the gift of tongues?

The gift of tongues has a few different subdivisions. The first is the ability to speak in foreign languages without learning them. This is seen in Acts 2, when the disciples were together at Pentecost.

> And they were all filled with the Holy Ghost, and began to speak with other tongues, as the Spirit gave them utterance. And there were dwelling at Jerusalem Jews, devout men, out of every nation under heaven. Now when this was noised abroad, the multitude came together, and were confounded, because that every man heard them speak in his own language. And they were all amazed and marvelled, saying one to another, Behold, are not all these which speak Galilaeans? And how hear we every man in our own tongue, wherein we were born? (Acts 2:5—8)

I don't know (and we can't know for sure) whether they were speaking in one language, but were heard in all other languages, or whether they were all speaking different languages. However, I do know that whichever it is, they could communicate God's message to everybody without any language barrier.

First Corinthians 14:9—11 says,

> So likewise ye, except ye utter by the tongue words easy to be understood, how

shall it be known what is spoken? for ye shall speak into the air. There are, it may be, so many kinds of voices in the world, and none of them is without signification. Therefore if I know not the meaning of the voice, I shall be unto him that speaketh a barbarian, and he that speaketh shall be a barbarian unto me.

Here we can conclude that the gift of tongues can be the ability to speak actual foreign languages. People in a church may understand one who is speaking in tongues if he or she is saying words that many of us know, such as "Hola" or "Bonjour." But if that person speaks beyond these well-known foreign words, their speech will be useless.

How does speaking in foreign tongues profit the Church? Well, in the beginning of the Church age, the disciples speaking in foreign languages caused the unsaved to marvel and give attention to the power of God. However, today it is much easier to learn another language, and thus it does not usually cause people to marvel. Speaking in foreign tongues profits the Church by being able to give the message of God to the foreign world and churches that include people who don't speak, for example, English. However, what is being spoken in a foreign tongue must be interpreted so that all can understand the message. Speaking in foreign tongues also aids the speaker by being able to communicate to others who speak a different language which may also in some way or another benefit or protect the one who is speaking in tongues.

This subdivision of tongues should only be used in a church as there is need (1 Corinthians 14:12). If it is done unnecessarily, it would only cause chaos and destruction to that church (1 Corinthians 14:23). Of course, the Holy Spirit will usually prompt you when to do it. When one does speak in tongues, that person must strive to do it in the most orderly fashion without seeking to gain attention for themselves (1 Corinthians 14:40). It also must be interpreted, either by the speaker or by one gifted with interpretation of tongues (1 Corinthians 14:28).

The second subdivision is speaking in an unknown tongue that no one in a particular group will be able to understand. This is seen in 1 Corinthians 14:21—22, which says,

> In the law it is written, With men of other tongues and other lips will I speak unto this people; and yet for all that will they not hear me, saith the Lord. Wherefore tongues are for a sign, not to them that believe, but to them that believe not.

This form of tongues is intended to be judgment on Israel specifically. As this passage states, even with this fulfilled prophecy (found in Isaiah 28:11—12), the Jews will still not turn to God.

This subdivision should not be used in a church, unless, probably, it is in Israel or where there are unbelieving Jews. But usually, unbelieving Jews would not be in churches. This is most likely for outside of a church.

The third subdivision is a divine language meant for the individual in his communion with God or expression of worship toward God. This can be found in 1 Corinthians 14:2 and 13—16:

> For he that speaketh in an unknown tongue speaketh not unto men, but unto God: for no man understandeth him; howbeit in the spirit he speaketh mysteries. Wherefore let him that speaketh in an unknown tongue pray that he may interpret. For if I pray in an unknown tongue, my spirit prayeth, but my understanding is unfruitful. What is it then? I will pray with the spirit, and I will pray with the understanding also: I will sing with the spirit, and I will sing with the understanding also. Else when thou shalt bless with the spirit, how shall he that occupieth the room of the unlearned say Amen at thy giving of thanks, seeing he understandeth not what thou sayest?

This can also be used in a church (as long as it is interpreted), but it is mainly used in the individual's prayer life. This tongue is not spoken unto men, but unto God.

What could possibly be the benefit of this gift? Well, for one, it edifies the individual. It brings him in closer communion with God and uplifts him and increases his faith in the invisible God. Also, the Spirit may cause one to pray for something specific that the individual does not know about. Romans 8:26—27 says,

> Likewise the Spirit also helpeth our infirmities: for we know not what we should pray for as we ought: but the Spirit

> itself maketh intercession for us with groanings which cannot be uttered. And he that searcheth the hearts knoweth what is the mind of the Spirit, because he maketh intercession for the saints according to the will of God.

Though the Holy Spirit does this for every believer, for some He does this in a greater degree. The people who pray in tongues are intercessors for the Church and for others. If the individual wants to know what he is praying for, he can ask of God for the interpretation. Sometimes, words can't adequately describe one's feelings towards God, which is why speaking in tongues comes in handy. It allows the Spirit to interpret the tongue to the Father.

Another benefit is the edification of the church. Verses 16—17 of 1 Corinthians 14 say,

> Else when thou shalt bless with the spirit, how shall he that occupieth the room of the unlearned say Amen at thy giving of thanks, seeing he understandeth not what thou sayest? For thou verily givest thanks well, but the other is not edified.

Of course, speaking in tongues can only uplift the church if it is interpreted. This use of speaking in tongues uplifts the church through the moving of the Spirit to give thanks and praise to God. Why can't it be in English (or whatever the language of the region is)? Probably because it signifies that the praise is coming from the Spirit and that He is abundantly present and pleased. As in prayer, it can also be because one has no words in their vocabulary to express themselves toward God, so they speak in an unknown tongue.

The gift of tongues may also serve as a sign of genuine salvation (specifically, the indwelling of the Holy Spirit). This is usually seen in revivals of a larger group (Acts 10:45—47, 19:6). It signifies to the preacher that his message was not of none effect. This is why at the great revivals in history, there were many who spoke out in tongues. It was a sign of fruit. I'm not suggesting, however, that everyone who is saved will be able to speak in tongues (though I'm sure they could if they desired to and asked God for it).

Why all the gibberish?

Permit me to expose something else regarding tongues. Many Cessationists would say that modern tongues-speaking is mere gibberish with no uniformity, which is true concerning the unknown, "heavenly" tongue. They may reason, however, that because there is no structure (for example, one person who is speaking in tongues may utter one sound for a certain word while another person speaking in tongues may utter a different sound for the same word), it cannot be an actual, heavenly language and must therefore be fake.

Though it is true that there is no structure in "tongues," that does not mean it is counterfeit. You see, God intended that it be undecipherable and untranslatable, which makes a lack of uniformity and structure necessary. It is indeed more of a combination of sounds than it is a language, but the emphasis of the gift isn't the sounds, per se, but the One behind the sounds—the Holy Spirit. The "gibberish" is meant to signify a moving of the Holy Spirit. It is the epitome of Romans 8:26.

Still Continuing

I would give the scriptural arguments Cessationists use to defend the cessation of the gift of tongues. However, there is one problem: They don't have any. They claim to have 1 Corinthians 13:8—12, but that only says that tongues will cease. It is unclear when it will cease. In Mark 16:17, Christ lists speaking in tongues as a sign that will develop in those that believe in general. Did He say that only those in the early Church age will be able to speak in tongues? No. Speaking in tongues will characterize those that believe, then and now. If speaking in tongues ended when the Scriptures were completed even though the Scriptures did not say it will end when it is complete, then we can easily conclude that all of the other gifts ended as well. After all, why not?

But one more question: When exactly did the gift of tongues cease: At the destruction of the Jerusalem temple, at the completion of the New Testament, or at the death of the last of the 12 Apostles? You argue that the destruction of the Jerusalem temple marked the end of the prior signs of judgment, including tongues; however, you also say that the sign gifts were dependent upon the completion of the Scriptures and ended when the Scriptures were completed. What's more, some of you also say that the signs gifts were only for the Apostles. The last of them died after 100 A.D.—years after the completion of Scripture, which was around 90 A.D.—20 years after the destruction of the Jerusalem temple. So when did the gift of tongues stop, and what was the gift dependent on? I believe that the gift is dependent on the Holy Spirit, who is still being poured out upon mankind, which means the gift of tongues is still being given.

9

Healing

What is the gift of healing?

The gift of healing is the ability given by the Spirit to heal someone. The Greek word for "healing" (*iama*) means "healing; curing." What is interesting is that Paul says that to one is given the *gifts* (plural) of healing. What this exactly implies I am not completely sure, but it is interesting to see. It may be that the gifts of healing are separated by the type of affliction that is healed. Maybe someone has the gift of healing for deformity, while another has the gift of healing for pain, and another has the gift of healing for sicknesses.

Can any believer administer healing?

Speaking about believers in general, Jesus says at the end of Mark 16:18, "They shall lay hands on the sick, and they shall recover." Anybody can heal someone in the Name of Jesus if done in faith that He will heal. Anybody can and should pray over one who is afflicted and plead with God for healing in Jesus'

Why Cessationism Can't Be True

name for the individual. In James 5:14—15, the elders are told to pray over the sick, and if it is in faith, the individual will be healed. We must not doubt when we pray for healing. Instead, we must believe not only that God *can* heal, but also that He *will* heal (Matthew 21:18—22).

What makes the gift of healing unique?

If any believer can perform healing, what makes the gifts of healing unique? Well, first of all, those with the gifts of healing have the special God-given desire for people's healing, which is the same with other gifts. Secondly, those with the gifts of healing specialize in the healing ministry. That is the area of ministry they focus on. Thirdly, though they don't override God's will, God does often use them as the instruments of healing. This can be applied to the gift of teaching and other gifts as well.

Are the ministries and gifts of healing still around? Well, I know that many people have been healed immediately through the prayers of a believer, and that many believers have immediately (through God's power) healed those who were afflicted. But Cessationists claim that the gift of healing does not exist anymore. Despite having no explicit scriptural support, they supposedly have implicit scriptural evidence.

What about Philippians 2:25—27, 1 Timothy 5:23, and 2 Timothy 4:20?

In the first passage, Epaphroditus was sick nigh unto death, and yet Paul did not heal him. In the second, Paul tells Timothy to take a little wine for his infirmities instead of healing him. In the third, Paul left Trophimus sick at Miletum. Why? If he had the gift of healing (as is seen in Acts), why didn't he heal his fellows? Cessationists say it is because he couldn't heal them, because he had lost the gift. But where is that in Scripture? It is only speculation.

The problem with their argument is that in Philippians, Epaphroditus was healed ("but God had mercy on him") and was able to go to Philippi. In 1 Timothy, Paul was imprisoned in Rome, and thus could not go to Timothy to lay hands on him and heal him. In 2 Timothy, Paul is talking about something in the past, possibly as much as 10 years earlier. He left Trophimus at Miletus sick. This was before the event at Malta in which Paul healed Publius' father and all the sick on that island. This event was recorded in the last chapter of the Book of Acts, ending on a strong note for the gift of healing. If Paul did not heal Trophimus, but still had the gift of healing (because he healed people even after he left Trophimus), how can we use the reasoning that because Paul did not heal someone, it means that he couldn't? Maybe there are other factors involved.

What about 2 Corinthians 12:7—9?

Here Paul had a thorn in the flesh (caused by Satan), and beseeched the Lord three times to remove it. God didn't remove it. Instead, He said to Paul that through this weakness His strength will be made perfect. With this, Cessationists say that Paul could not heal himself (he lost the gift), and instead of healing, God uses affliction to mold his disciples.

There are a few problems with this reasoning. The first is that Paul knew he had the gift, and did what he normally did to heal others. He prayed (the word used in this passage literally means "to implore; invoke") that God would let the affliction depart from him. So Paul was not aware, at least, that he lost the gift. Second, this was before the healings done on Malta. So he lost the gift? Not at all!

Third, if God was using affliction and not healing for molding his disciples, why did he give the gifts of healing anyway? Why would He all-of-a-sudden change from healing people through His disciples (and not healing as well) to not healing people through His disciples at all? The reasoning that "God does not wish for His disciples to heal his children anymore because He is instead using affliction" is nonsense because He was still using affliction from the very beginning. And that reasoning does not make sense with the fact that God did indeed give the gifts of healing to certain believers. Why did He give that gift in the first place?

Also, is the thorn in the flesh a medical condition? When you look at the verse (v. 7), Paul specifies the thorn in the flesh. He said it was "the messenger of Satan to buffet me." God used these taunts from a demon to keep him from becoming proud. We can't be sure what the thorn was, but we also can't assume it was a medical condition.

Still Continuing

Where do the Scriptures actually state or even imply that the gifts of healing ceased? It doesn't. Then why do Cessationists believe that the gift ceased? The only reason I can think of is because they want to believe that the gift ceased. They can argue using human reasoning, but they know that it has no significance when we are dealing with God's truth. If His Word does not affirm that view, that view must be rejected. Do not elevate experience above God's Word.

James 5:14—15 says,

> Is any sick among you? let him call for the elders of the church; and let them pray over him, anointing him with oil in the name of the Lord: And the prayer of faith shall save the sick, and the Lord shall raise him up; and if he have committed sins, they shall be forgiven him.

If you don't believe that this text still applies today, then you must be consistent and believe that the surrounding text does not apply today. That includes the verses that say,

> Is any among you afflicted? let him pray. Is any merry? let him sing psalms... Confess your faults one to another, and pray one for another, that ye may be healed. The effectual fervent prayer of a righteous man availeth much. (James 5:13,16)

Why Cessationism Can't Be True

Permit me to conclude this chapter with these verses:

> And these signs shall follow them that believe...they shall lay hands on the sick, and they shall recover. (Mark 16:17—18)

> Heal the sick, cleanse the lepers, raise the dead, cast out devils: freely ye have received, freely give. (Matthew 10:8)

10

Miracles

What is the gift of working miracles?

The word "miracle" in the Greek is *"dunamis"*, and means "force; power; ability." A miracle is a supernatural phenomenon or experience. One of the gifts given by the Spirit is the working of miracles. This gift probably includes miracles similar to what Christ did.

What is the purpose of working miracles?

Miracles are performed in a believer through the power of God to increase faith in other believers and promote fear for God and awe for Him. There are other purposes for this gift that are relative to the individual who is receiving or witnessing the miracle, or relative to the situation at hand.

What about demonic power?

There are people who can perform miracles by the power of demons (1 Timothy 4:1, Matthew 24:24). Just because one performs miracles, it does not mean that they are doing it by the Holy Spirit's power. But there are miracles that can't be performed by demons, for even they are limited in power. Miracles have been performed by both Satan's power and God's power since the beginning of time, practically.

Can any believer work miracles?

Matthew 21:18—21 says,

> Now in the morning as he returned into the city, he hungered. And when he saw a fig tree in the way, he came to it, and found nothing thereon, but leaves only, and said unto it, Let no fruit grow on thee henceforward forever. And presently the fig tree withered away. And when the disciples saw it, they marvelled, saying, How soon is the fig tree withered away! Jesus answered and said unto them, Verily I say unto you, If ye have faith, and doubt not, ye shall not only do this which is done to the fig tree, but also if ye shall say unto this mountain, Be thou removed, and be thou cast into the sea; it shall be done.

If we have the faith, we can perform the miracles Christ did. How? Because we have the Holy Spirit within us. Christ said in John 14:12,

> Verily, verily, I say unto you, He that believeth on me, the works that I do shall he do also; and greater works than these shall he do; because I go unto my Father.

Working miracles is something any believer can do if they have faith, but those with the gift of working miracles specialize and excel in it for the profit of the Church.

What about false prophets working miracles?

Some say that because false prophets work miracles, Christians do not work miracles through the Spirit. They reason that because false prophets work in the outward appearance, performing wonders and miracles, genuine believers performing miracles would be a distraction from the Spirit's work in the souls of unbelievers. However, there were unbelievers performing miracles even in the early days of the Church (Acts 8:9, 13:6), so that reasoning is invalid. They might also say that since the Bible says that miracles will be performed through false prophets (Matthew 24:24), then whoever is performing miracles today are false prophets. Again, that reasoning is invalid because it occurred in Paul's day. And just because false prophets will perform miracles in these last days, it does not mean that all who perform miracles in these last days are false prophets. That's like saying, "Since dogs walk on all fours, then every animal that walks on all fours is a dog." It's a logical fallacy.

Still Continuing

There is no scriptural argument Cessationists use to defend the cessation of the gift of working miracles. Again, I want to ask them, "Why would you still believe it?" Christ said in John 14:12,

> Verily, verily, I say unto you, He that believeth on me, the works that I do shall he do also; and greater works than these shall he do; because I go unto my Father.

Whoever believes, from those in the past to those in the present to those in the future, will do the works that Christ did. As a matter of fact, they will do greater works than He. How? Christ went to the Father and beseeched Him to give us the Holy Spirit and those gifts. If you believe in Christ, then what He said in John 14:12 applies to you.

11

Cooperation of the Gifts

Before I explain, let me allow you to read the passage from which I am building this chapter on, found in 1 Corinthians 12.

> For as the body is one, and hath many members, and all the members of that one body, being many, are one body: so also is Christ. For by one Spirit are we all baptized into one body, whether we be Jews or Gentiles, whether we be bond or free; and have been all made to drink into one Spirit. For the body is not one member, but many. If the foot shall say, Because I am not the hand, I am not of the body; is it therefore not of the body? And if the ear shall say, Because I am not the eye, I am not of the body; is it therefore not of the body? If the whole body were an eye, where were the hearing? If the whole were hearing, where were the smelling?

But now hath God set the members every one of them in the body, as it hath pleased him. And if they were all one member, where were the body? But now are they many members, yet but one body. And the eye cannot say unto the hand, I have no need of thee: nor again the head to the feet, I have no need of you. Nay, much more those members of the body, which seem to be more feeble, are necessary: And those members of the body, which we think to be less honorable, upon these we bestow more abundant honor; and our uncomely parts have more abundant comeliness.

For our comely parts have no need: but God hath tempered the body together, having given more abundant honor to that part which lacked: That there should be no schism in the body; but that the members should have the same care one for another. And whether one member suffer, all the members suffer with it; or one member be honored, all the members rejoice with it. Now ye are the body of Christ, and members in particular. (1 Corinthians 12:12—27)

Let's first discuss the unity of the gifts. Various saints have various gifts. There is not one gift that every believer has. Neither is there a believer who has all the gifts. All these gifts are intended to harmonize with each other so that the body of Christ can be edified and benefited. It is the Holy Spirit who works through each one of us, performing these gifts in us. We are all united under the Spirit. We are one body, with various parts to perform various functions.

Lacking a certain gift does not make a believer not part of the body. The foot does not need to be a hand to be part of the body. The ear does not need to be an eye to be part of the body. Just imagine a body that could only see, and couldn't smell, hear, touch. That would make it hard for the body to function at its best. It would also look strange, no doubt. Just because you don't have a certain gift, that does not make you disqualified from the body. Your gift is useful and beneficial.

All of the gifts are necessary. We must not dare say that a certain gift is not necessary or important. Actually, those gifts that appear to be less important are more necessary than you think. There were some parts of the human body that scientists thought were unnecessary, but they were actually quite significant. There are gifts of the body of Christ that some people think are unnecessary, and some go even so far as to say they don't belong to the body anymore. They are wrong, for all of the various members are necessary. God has given more honor to the seemingly unnecessary gifts so that there would be no division in the body.

The doctrine of Cessationism has caused huge division within the Church. Churches have vomited many members of the body out. Thus, there are believers who are not accepted in the church because of their gifts. If someone speaks in tongues, they tell them to stop because the gift has ceased. If someone prophesies, they tell them to stop because the gift has ceased. If someone lays their hands on someone to heal, they tell them to stop because the gift has ceased. This forces the believers with those gifts to form their own denomination. Then, because many believers who don't have the "sign gifts" believe the "sign gifts" have ceased, the "Charismatic" churches are sometimes left incomplete, because they don't have the other members of the body. This makes both sides incomplete, inefficient, and pathetic.

> Endeavoring to keep the unity of the Spirit in the bond of peace. There is one body, and one Spirit, even as ye are called in one hope of your calling. (Ephesians 4:3—4)

It is crucial that all the gifts remain in the body, for if "one member suffer, all the members suffer with it" (1 Corinthians 12:26).

12

1 Corinthians 13:8–12

First Corinthians 13:8—12 says,

> Charity never fails: but whether there be prophecies, they shall fail; whether there be tongues, they shall cease; whether there be knowledge, it shall vanish away. For we know in part, and we prophesy in part. But when that which is perfect is come, then that which is in part shall be done away. When I was a child, I spoke as a child, I understood as a child, I thought as a child: but when I became a man, I put away childish things. For now we see through a glass, darkly; but then face to face: now I know in part; but then shall I know even as also I am known.

This passage is the key to the answer of whether the "sign gifts" have already ceased. The problem is that the interpretation of the passage is debated between Cessationists and Continuationists. I have already exposed the faultiness in the Cessationist interpretation, and I would encourage you to go back to that section ("Arguments Refuted") to review those flaws. The basic conflict between the interpretation of the Cessationists and the Continuationists is whether the gifts mentioned will end with the completion of Scripture or when we are glorified. Both views can make sense of this passage. Every section in this passage, however, points to when we are with Christ if read naturally and without presuppositions. That is what I am intending to show you. The interpretation is actually quite obvious if examined unbiasedly.

> Charity never fails. (1 Corinthians 13:8a)

Never means never. In the context of chapters 12—14, Paul is not condemning the spiritual gifts. He actually commends and encourages them. He is emphasizing the importance of exercising these gifts in love, instead of pride and selfishness. Love is more important than the gifts, because it is eternal and will go into eternity. Unlike the gifts, love will never end.

> Whether there be prophecies, they shall fail; whether there be tongues, they shall cease; whether there be knowledge, it shall vanish away. (1 Corinthians 13:8b)

The literal translation of the Greek would say,

> Whether there be prophecies, they shall become useless; whether there be tongues they shall cease; whether there be knowledge, it shall become useless.

There are three gifts mentioned: prophecy, tongues, and knowledge. Prophecy and knowledge are said to become useless, whereas the gift of tongues is said to cease. Why the difference? Paul explains the difference in the next verses up to the very end of the chapter. Before we discuss those next verses, I'll give an illustration, using parentheses to show the analogies.

You work a night-time shift at a construction site (this current life), and the boss gives you a hammer (gift of tongues) and special night-vision goggles (gifts of prophecy and knowledge). Then you get promoted to work a day-time shift as an office worker (when the perfect comes). You don't need your night-vision goggles (gifts of prophecy and knowledge) anymore because you can see clearly without them now. The hammer (gift of tongues) ceases to be yours because you don't need it anymore; not because you can bang in nails just as fine without the hammer, but because the job you have now ceases to require a hammer. A hammer is still useful, but not for your job. Night-vision goggles, however, would be useless, because, what good would it do if you could see clearly in the daylight? You see the difference? The gift of tongues is aiding you in doing a temporary job, but the gifts of prophecy and knowledge aid you in doing something you will be doing in completeness when you see the Lord, so the aid won't be necessary at that time.

> For we know in part, and we prophesy in part. (1 Corinthians 13:9)

Even with the gifts, we only know in part and prophesy in part. Those gifts are partial. Are you complete in knowledge? Can you see and predict every future event? I would admit that I can't, and I know that you can't. That means, then, that your knowledge is partial and your prophecy is partial.

Proverbs 30:3—4 says,

> I neither learned wisdom, nor have the knowledge of the holy. Who hath ascended up into heaven, or descended? who hath gathered the wind in his fists? who hath bound the waters in a garment? who hath established all the ends of the earth? what is his name, and what is his son's name, if thou canst tell?

Job 11:7—8 says,

> Canst thou by searching find out God? canst thou find out the Almighty unto perfection? It is as high as heaven; what canst thou do? deeper than hell; what canst thou know?

We don't know and can't know everything, but we can know many things because of the Holy Spirit dwelling within us. Chapters earlier in 1 Corinthians 2:11, Paul says,

> Now we have received, not the spirit of the world, but the spirit which is of God; that we might know the things that are freely given to us of God.

But even with that, he says, "For we know in part,

and we prophesy in part." Can anyone disagree with that?

To make this distinction between the gifts of knowledge and prophecy and the gift of tongues, let me give a visual. Imagine three pie charts: one is the gift of knowledge, one is the gift of prophecy, and one is the gift of tongues. The pie charts for knowledge and prophecy are 20% complete, so they are currently incomplete pie charts. The pie chart for tongues, however, is completely filled. Someday, the pie charts for knowledge and prophecy will become complete at 100%. The partial gifts of knowledge and prophecy will one day become complete, which will then render the gifts useless. The pie chart for tongues, however, will go all the way to 0%. It will end instead of being fulfilled. That's because tongues is no longer applicable in heaven. All three gifts will become unnecessary someday, but two of them will become useless while the other becomes inapplicable.

> But when that which is perfect is come,
> then that which is in part shall be done away. (1 Corinthians 13:10)

There will be a point in time when the partial gifts will become useless and be done away, which is when the perfect comes. What is the "perfect" referring to? First, notice that it is the opposite of "partial." There is a complete and an incomplete. A natural exegesis is that the incomplete gifts will be done away when the complete gifts come (which obviously would only be when we are in heaven or when Christ returns). The ISV (International Standard Version) translation makes this interpretation clearer to see:

> But when what is complete comes, then what is incomplete will be done away with.

This is probably the only interpretation the Corinthians would have had for what Paul said. Otherwise, why would he be so vague? The only other possible interpretation that is sensible and would not be deceiving to the Corinthians (or to us, for that matter) would be that the "perfect" is referring to perfectness, or maturity. When we become perfect and fully mature, the partial gifts will be done away. Our knowledge would be perfect, so we wouldn't need the gift of knowledge. Our foresight of the future would be perfect, so we wouldn't need the gift of prophecy. I lean more toward the first interpretation; but either way, the only reasonable interpretations both point to when we are in heavenly bodies.

> When I was a child, I spoke as a child, I understood as a child, I thought as a child: but when I became a man, I put away childish things. (1 Corinthians 13:11)

Here Paul uses an analogy to explain the doing away of the gifts. When he was a child, he spoke as a child (gift of tongues), understood as a child (gift of knowledge), and thought as a child (gift of prophecy). But when he became a man, he put away those childish things (the gifts of tongues, knowledge, and prophecy). So we know that the gifts are done away when the perfect comes, so "Paul becoming a man" must equate with "the perfect coming."

Paul had the childish things, just as we have the gifts. The childish things were put away, just as the gifts will be done away with. The doing away with the childish things happened when the possessor of those childish things (Paul) became a man (fully mature). Thus, the doing away with the gifts will happen when the possessors of those gifts (us) become fully mature. That could only be when we receive the complete gifts of knowledge and prophecy as opposed to the incomplete gifts of knowledge and prophecy, which is only when we are glorified. The perfect can't be referring to the completion of Scripture, because (though it became complete) it did not possess those childish things (the gifts).

> For now we see through a glass, darkly;
> but then face to face. (1 Corinthians 13:12a)

The Greek word for "glass" can also mean "mirror," which is what Cessationists tend to prefer. They like the word "mirror" because the Word of God is a mirror (James 1:23—25). They point to James 1:23 as a relation to 1 Corinthians 13:12; however, this glass does not reference the Scriptures. It is very likely referring to just the fact that life currently is like looking through a foggy window, which is what I have traditionally thought throughout my entire lifetime. Besides, the word "through" cannot be referring to a mirror.

Eventually, there will be a time that we will see face to face. See whom face to face? Ourselves? No. The term "face to face" is never used in the Bible to refer to a reflection. Out of the 11 times the phrase is used,

10 of them obviously don't refer to a reflection (e.g., Judges 6:22 and 3 John 1:14). Would the phrase in 1 Corinthians 13:12 be the only phrase that refers to a reflection? Not at all! I never say "face to face" when I want to refer to seeing myself in a reflection. I do say "face to face" when I want to refer to seeing someone face to face. Remember the hymn "Face to Face"?

> Face to face with Christ, my Savior,
> Face to face—what will it be,
> When with rapture I behold Him,
> Jesus Christ who died for me?
>
> Only faintly now, I see Him,
> With the darkling veil between,
> But a blessed day is coming,
> When His glory shall be seen.
>
> What rejoicing in His presence,
> When are banished grief and pain;
> When the crooked ways are straightened,
> And the dark things shall be plain.
>
> Face to face! O blissful moment!
> Face to face—to see and know;
> Face to face with my Redeemer,
> Jesus Christ who loves me so.
>
> CHORUS:
>
> Face to face I shall behold Him,
> Far beyond the starry sky;
> Face to face in all His glory,
> I shall see Him by and by!

Compare 1 Corinthians 13:12 with 1 John 3:2 and 1 Corinthians 4:5.

> For now we see through a glass, darkly; but then face to face: now I know in part; but then shall I know even as also I am known. (1 Corinthians 13:12)

> Beloved, now are we the sons of God, and it doth not yet appear what we shall be: but we know that, when he shall appear, we shall be like him; for we shall see him as he is. (1 John 3:2)

> Therefore judge nothing before the time, until the Lord come, who both will bring to light the hidden things of darkness, and will make manifest the counsels of the hearts: and then shall every man have praise of God. (1 Corinthians 4:5)

> Now I know in part; but then shall I know even as also I am known. (1 Corinthians 13:12b)

Paul says that he only knows in part. Even after God revealed truth to him (Galatians 1:11—12), and even though he wrote the majority of the New Testament and had the opportunity to hear the teaching of the 12 Apostles, he still admitted that he only knew in part. I don't think any honest person would claim or even think that he knows as much as Paul knew. So if Paul only knew in part, how much more we, who don't even have as much knowledge as Paul? However, there

Why Cessationism Can't Be True

will be a time when we will know as we are known. Known of whom? The only answer could be God. Do you know as much as you are known of God? I don't, and certainly you don't.

One way we can determine the meaning of a passage is by comparing with other Scripture passages that are clearer. In Ephesians 4:11—12, we see that God has given certain offices, including prophets, "for the perfecting of the saints, for the work of the ministry, for the edifying of the body of Christ." In verse 13, we see for how long these gifts will be given to the Church, including the gift of prophecy. It says,

> Till we all come in the unity of the faith,
> and of the knowledge of the Son of God,
> unto a perfect man, unto the measure of
> the stature of the fullness of Christ.

Are the saints unified in the faith and the knowledge of the Son of God? Are the saints perfect, complete, and fully mature? Do the saints measure up to Christ's stature, or to the stature of His completeness? The answer to these questions is an emphatic "no." If the answer were "yes," then we wouldn't need pastors or teachers either. But we do, because we are not yet complete and mature.

The only time when we will be complete and mature is when we are glorified. So if the office of prophet was given until that time, it has not ceased to be given yet. Some say, "Well we have their words in the Scriptures." Well we also have the words of pastors and teachers and evangelists. And we don't have the words of all the prophets. If the gift of prophet/prophecy has not ceased to be given, then that means that 1 Corinthians

13:8—12 cannot be implying that the gift of prophecy will end when the Scriptures are completed. Rather, it is referring to the glorification of the Church. And because that is true, the other gifts mentioned with prophecy will not cease until the glorification of the Church.

Now read the passage again:

> Charity never fails: but whether there be prophecies, they shall fail; whether there be tongues, they shall cease; whether there be knowledge, it shall vanish away. For we know in part, and we prophesy in part. But when that which is perfect is come, then that which is in part shall be done away. When I was a child, I spoke as a child, I understood as a child, I thought as a child: but when I became a man, I put away childish things. For now we see through a glass, darkly; but then face to face: now I know in part; but then shall I know even as also I am known. (1 Corinthians 13:8—12)

Each part in this passage points to our glorification, not to the completion of the Scriptures. Thus, the gifts of knowledge, prophecy, and tongues will end when we are glorified. If the gifts of prophecy and tongues ended with the completion of the Scriptures, then the gift of knowledge ended with the completion of the Scriptures as well (which some agree to, while others do not).

13

Scriptural Authority

A big problem with the Cessationist view is that it forgets that doctrine must be based on the explicit teachings of Scripture. Yes, of course they use the Scriptures. Almost all false doctrines that invade Christianity use the Scriptures as "support." There is always a passage that they pull out to back up their claims, yet pulled out of proportion. Cessationism is not much different than the other erroneous beliefs, because it ignores the rest of Scripture and relies mostly on human reasoning and logic.

We must not base our doctrines on human reasoning. Rather, we must base our doctrines on *Sola Scriptura* (Scripture Alone). Try giving only Scripture passages (without explanation) to support Cessationism—you can't! Where in the Bible does it explicitly say that the gift of healings ceased? Where in the Bible does it explicitly say that the gift of miracles ceased? What about the gift of discerning between spirits? What about the gift of wisdom? Cessationists don't even have one verse that says anything about those gifts ceasing. Then how do they "know" that those gifts have ceased? The answer: By speculation and human reasoning.

They are just like Evolutionists, who only rely on "educated guesses." However, it is clearly in opposition to the teachings of Scripture. Do Cessationists have scriptural support for the cessation of the gifts of apostleship, prophecy, tongues, and knowledge? Not really. They have to twist everything to direct it towards their belief. And, as we saw earlier, their interpretations are completely faulty.

Would any believer fresh to the Word of God come to the conclusion that some of the gifts of the Spirit have already ceased, by reading through the New Testament (or even the whole Bible)? I doubt it. When I hear advocates of Cessationism defend their belief, I rarely hear Scripture. They are mostly rambling on with all kinds of human reasoning and logic. If you ask them to give one reason why certain gifts have ceased, they will almost never reply with a Scripture passage. If they do, they have to add assumptions (that are flimsy and defenseless when challenged) to make the passage support their belief. How can one ever know that Cessationism is true if it has no explicit Scripture as a foundation?

The Scriptures are sufficient for truth. If it takes going beyond Scripture to back up a theological view, then that view is not truth. We must rely on the Scriptures alone, and no other. We must be students of the Word, not masters of it. Our theology must change as we discover truth in God's Word, for what can be more reliable?

14

Commands Concerning the Gifts

Did you know that most Cessationists believe that we must obey and follow every New Testament command? However, they make an exception for the commands concerning the gifts of tongues, prophecy, and healing. The commands concerning those gifts are often the only commands they believe we shouldn't follow anymore. They reason that it is because of the change of times, but can't we say that about other commands? And, believe me, some have. It does not make sense that Cessationists would go so far as to violate explicit commands in the New Testament.

> Having then gifts differing according to the grace that is given to us, whether prophecy, let us prophesy according to the proportion of faith. (Romans 12:6)

> As every man hath received the gift, even so minister the same one to another, as

> good stewards of the manifold grace of God. (1 Peter 4:10)
>
> Wherefore, brethren, covet to prophesy, and forbid not to speak with tongues. (1 Corinthians 14:39)
>
> Despise not prophesyings. (1 Thessalonians 5:20)
>
> Heal the sick, cleanse the lepers, raise the dead, cast out devils: freely ye have received, freely give. (Matthew 10:8)

These commands were not for a specific group, but for all believers. Paul goes so far as to say,

> If any man thinks himself to be a prophet, or spiritual, let him acknowledge that the things that I write unto you are the commandments of the Lord. But if any man be ignorant, let him be ignorant. (1 Corinthians 14:37—38)

Romans 12:6 and 1 Peter 4:10 command us to use the gifts God has given us. First Corinthians 14:39 commands us to desire to prophesy. It also commands us not to forbid speaking in tongues. That means that you should not refuse to speak in tongues if the Spirit urges you to do so and you should not to prohibit others from speaking in tongues.

Do you know of anyone or any churches that prohibit people from speaking in tongues? Well, we can apply what Paul said in 1 Corinthians 14:37—38 to that church or person.

Jeremiah 8:8—9 says,

> How can you claim, 'We are wise; the law of the LORD is with us'? In fact, the lying pen of scribes has produced falsehood. The wise will be put to shame; they will be dismayed and snared. They have rejected the word of the LORD, so what wisdom do they really have?

If it isn't explicitly taught, don't believe any doctrine that violates any commands of God.

15

Reality Concerning the Gifts

If these "sign gifts" have ceased after the completion of the New Testament, how were there Christians who had those gifts in the past? And how are there Christians with these gifts today?

> Then remembered I the word of the Lord, how that he said, John indeed baptized with water; but ye shall be baptized with the Holy Ghost. Forasmuch then as God gave them the like gift as he did unto us, who believed on the Lord Jesus Christ; what was I, that I could withstand God? When they heard these things, they held their peace, and glorified God, saying, Then hath God also to the Gentiles granted repentance unto life. (Acts 11:15—18)

At first the disciples of Christ thought that salvation was only for the Jews. But when Peter told them about the vision he received, and how that the Gentiles received the Holy Spirit when he preached to them, the disciples accepted the fact that "then hath God also to the Gentiles granted repentance unto life." They were willing to accept what they hadn't accepted at first, because they could not reject the fact that the Gentiles did indeed receive the indwelling of the Holy Spirit. As Peter said,

> Now if God gave them the same gift that he gave us when we believed in the Lord Jesus, the Messiah, who was I to try to stop God? (Acts 11:17, ISV).

You see, we must be willing to accept whatever God does. The positive outweighs the negative. If someone says that dinosaurs do not exist anymore, and someone finds even just one dinosaur, then that negates the entire presupposition that dinosaurs do not exist anymore. If someone says there are no stars in the sky, and someone else sees a star in the sky, then there are indeed stars in the sky. The positive outweighs the negative. A generalization can easily be refuted if even one evidence is contrary to it.

The same can be applied to the existence of the "sign gifts." Most Cessationists claim that record and reality show that those gifts have ceased since the end of the Apostolic Age. They point to all the Church fathers who stated that those gifts are not seen to be exercised and have ceased. They point to today, and say, "There are no genuine Christians exercising the genuine 'sign gifts'; therefore, those gifts have ceased." That is the negative aspect. However, there is a positive aspect that points directly toward the existence of these gifts. Here are just a few of the early Church fathers and recent Christians who have (or have witnessed) these "sign gifts."

The first is Justin Martyr (c.100-165 A.D.), who acknowledged the continuation of all the gifts of the Spirit, including tongues and healings. He acknowledged that signs and miracles are still being done by believers, including demons being cast out. He also acknowledged that prophets were still in function.

The second is Irenaeus (c.130-200 A.D.), who testified that believers were still casting out demons, prophesying, receiving visions, healing the sick by the laying on of hands, even raising the dead, and speaking in tongues.

The third is Basil the Great (330-379 A.D.). He claimed that God is still active in gifts of healing and raising the dead.

The fourth is Augustine (354-430 A.D.). You might be like, "Wait a minute, he said himself that certain gifts have ceased." You're right. He did advocate the cessation of the "sign gifts." However, there was a point in time when he witnessed believers performing miracles. It was after that time that he changed his view on the gifts, and advocated the continuation of the gift of working miracles, though he did not believe they were exercised in the same degree that the early apostles performed miracles (i.e. people being healed when Peter's shadow passed by).

The fifth is Saint Patrick of Ireland. He obviously had the gift of prophecy. I have read his autobiographies, and how he had predicted many events in detail that were all fulfilled. He was definitely a Christian, and he prophesied, and his prophecies were fulfilled.

George Wishart was the mentor of the great reformer, John Knox. Wishart (a martyr of the faith) would prophesy many times in his ministry, usually against the people he was preaching to. In one case that I read of in Knox's biography of Wishart, he mentioned specific plagues that would invade the people he preached to. These exact plagues soon arrived into their city. John Knox affirmed in his own words that George Wishart had the gift of prophecy.

John Knox of Scotland was another Church leader who had the gift of prophecy. I have read his autobiographies, and how that he too had predicted many outcomes, all of which had turned out as truth.

One well-known scholar and teacher, Dr. Michael L. Brown, has the gift of tongues. He is definitely a Christian, and he cares only for what the Bible says when it comes to truth. He was raised in a Jewish home, so he wasn't an early Christian. He believes that the gift of tongues is still given to believers today, and he even has the gift himself. Many other Christians have the gift as well (just go to a faithful Charismatic church, and you'll find out for yourself). There's also Dr. Sam Storms (a former Cessationist) who prays in tongues. There are other genuine Christians I know of who speak in tongues as well.

Though most of the popular healers you find on the website are false prophets and false apostles, there are still believers who have healed individuals (including myself) and have the gift of healing. Check out the ministry Christ for All Nations at cfan.org and observe the many miracles of healing done through that ministry and the evangelist Daniel Kolenda. Deaf ears and blind eyes open, the lame walk again, the sick recover instantly, and even the dead come back to life. Other men of the recent past and the present who have performed miracles and healings include Smith Wigglesworth, John Wimbur, Randy Clark,

Todd White, and Robby Dawkins. There are many more as well.

I do know of a missionary who has preached at the church I was raised up in. It is recorded in his biography that he has cast out demons and healed people. He was definitely a Christian, yet he had been witnessed to do what Cessationists believe are impossible. But how could they think that? Didn't Christ say that exorcism and healing will accompany those that believe in Mark 16:17—18? He said in Luke 10:19,

> Behold, I give unto you power to tread on serpents and scorpions, and over all the power of the enemy: and nothing shall by any means hurt you.

Why are you blinding your eyes toward these evidences? You saw in the earlier sections how that your arguments are invalid, and you saw the overwhelming proofs that all the gifts are still being given, and now you have seen that there are genuine Christians who have the gifts that Cessationists believe have ceased. I know it confuses Cessationists. Why don't you just give up that rebellious doctrine of Cessationism, and turn to the doctrine that is taught in the Scriptures. You are seeing only what you want to see. Why don't you just see what is visible—both in the Scriptures and in reality?

Note: I have not cited my evidence for the statements made in this chapter. That's because it isn't necessary to refute Cessationism, and I don't care much of what you think of this chapter, because the evidence presented in this chapter is not scriptural evidence.

16

A Word About Visions

I am sure we agree that the men of God in the Old Testament received visions and dreams, specifically prophets. God often communicated a message to them through a vision. A vision can be in the form of a voice in the ears, a dream during one's sleep, or an actual appearance of the spiritual or future.

The prophet Joel prophesied,

> And it shall come to pass afterward, that I will pour out my spirit upon all flesh; and your sons and your daughters shall prophesy, your old men shall dream dreams, your young men shall see visions: And also upon the servants and upon the handmaids in those days will I pour out my spirit. And I will shew wonders in the heavens and in the earth, blood, and fire, and pillars of smoke. The sun shall be turned into darkness, and the moon into blood, before the great and the terrible day of the LORD come. And it shall come

> to pass, that whosoever shall call on the name of the LORD shall be delivered: for in mount Zion and in Jerusalem shall be deliverance, as the LORD hath said, and in the remnant whom the LORD shall call. (Joel 2:28—32)

Before the great day of the Lord, God will pour out His Spirit, and His people will prophesy, see visions, and dream dreams. When the Spirit poured onto the disciples gathered in Jerusalem at Pentecost, Peter testified in Acts 2:16—21,

> But this is that which was spoken by the prophet Joel; And it shall come to pass in the last days, saith God, I will pour out of my Spirit upon all flesh: and your sons and your daughters shall prophesy, and your young men shall see visions, and your old men shall dream dreams: And on my servants and on my handmaidens I will pour out in those days of my Spirit; and they shall prophesy: And I will shew wonders in heaven above, and signs in the earth beneath; blood, and fire, and vapour of smoke: The sun shall be turned into darkness, and the moon into blood, before that great and notable day of the Lord come: And it shall come to pass, that whosoever shall call on the name of the Lord shall be saved.

When does this prophecy say it will end? All it says is that it will happen before the great day of the Lord.

Why Cessationism Can't Be True

So if anything, it will end when Christ comes back. So where do we get the notion that God's people don't receive visions anymore? They get it from the idea that God now speaks to us through the Scriptures, and not through visions and dreams as He did with the Old Testament prophets and kings, and the Apostles of the early Church age. Now that the Scriptures are complete, they say, there is no need for more visions. They use Hebrews 1:1—2 as further support, which says,

> God, who at sundry times and in divers manners spake in time past unto the fathers by the prophets, Hath in these last days spoken unto us by his Son, whom he hath appointed heir of all things, by whom also he made the worlds.

Yes, God does speak to us through His Word, but that doesn't mean He doesn't also speak to us through visions and dreams. All throughout the New Testament, men received visions and dreams from God. I think another look at these visions will guide you toward the truth.

The first vision is found in Acts 9:1—18:

> And Saul, yet breathing out threatenings and slaughter against the disciples of the Lord, went unto the high priest, And desired of him letters to Damascus to the synagogues, that if he found any of this way, whether they were men or women, he might bring them bound unto Jerusalem. And as he journeyed,

he came near Damascus: and suddenly there shined round about him a light from heaven: And he fell to the earth, and heard a voice saying unto him, Saul, Saul, why persecutest thou me? And he said, Who art thou, Lord? And the Lord said, I am Jesus whom thou persecutest: it is hard for thee to kick against the pricks.

And he trembling and astonished said, Lord, what wilt thou have me to do? And the Lord said unto him, Arise, and go into the city, and it shall be told thee what thou must do. And the men which journeyed with him stood speechless, hearing a voice, but seeing no man. And Saul arose from the earth; and when his eyes were opened, he saw no man: but they led him by the hand, and brought him into Damascus. And he was three days without sight, and neither did eat nor drink.

And there was a certain disciple at Damascus, named Ananias; and to him said the Lord in a vision, Ananias. And he said, Behold, I am here, Lord. And the Lord said unto him, Arise, and go into the street which is called Straight, and enquire in the house of Judas for one called Saul, of Tarsus: for, behold, he prayeth, And hath seen in a vision a man named Ananias coming in, and putting his hand on him, that he might receive his sight. Then Ananias answered, Lord, I have heard by many of this man, how much evil he hath done to thy saints at Jerusalem: And here he hath authority from the chief priests to bind all that call on thy name. But the Lord said unto him, Go thy way: for he is a chosen vessel unto me, to bear my name before the Gentiles, and kings, and the children of Israel: For I will shew him how great things he must suffer for my name's sake.

And Ananias went his way, and entered into the house; and putting his hands on him said, Brother Saul, the Lord, even Jesus, that appeared unto thee in the way as thou camest, hath sent me, that thou mightest receive thy sight, and be filled with the Holy Ghost. And immediately there fell from his eyes as it had been scales: and he received sight forthwith, and arose, and was baptized.

Two visions are received in this passage. The first was to Saul, who later became Paul. Saul was so stubborn against Christ and the Gospel that God had to intervene supernaturally by means of a vision. This vision was personal, and was used to convert a defiant Pharisee who thought he was doing God's will. The second vision was to Ananias, and ordinary follower of Jesus Christ. This vision was given by God for instructions. In both cases, the vision was in an audible form.

Another vision is in Acts 10:9—20:

> On the morrow, as they went on their journey, and drew nigh unto the city, Peter went up upon the housetop to pray about the sixth hour: And he became very hungry, and would have eaten: but while they made ready, he fell into a trance, And saw heaven opened, and a certain vessel descending unto him, as it had been a great sheet knit at the four corners, and let down to the earth: Wherein were all manner of fourfooted beasts of the earth, and wild beasts, and creeping things, and fowls of the air. And there came a voice to him, Rise, Peter; kill, and eat. But Peter said, Not so, Lord; for I have never eaten anything that is common or unclean. And the voice spake unto him again the second time, What God hath cleansed, that call not thou common. This was done thrice: and the vessel was received up again into heaven.
>
> Now while Peter doubted in himself what this vision which he had seen should mean, behold, the men which were sent from Cornelius had made enquiry for Simon's house, and stood before the gate, And called, and asked whether Simon, which was surnamed Peter, were lodged there. While Peter thought on the vision, the Spirit said unto him, Behold, three men seek thee. Arise therefore, and get

thee down, and go with them, doubting nothing: for I have sent them.

Here is the same vision being recounted in Acts 11:4—12:

> But Peter rehearsed the matter from the beginning, and expounded it by order unto them, saying, I was in the city of Joppa praying: and in a trance I saw a vision, A certain vessel descend, as it had been a great sheet, let down from heaven by four corners; and it came even to me: Upon the which when I had fastened mine eyes, I considered, and saw four-footed beasts of the earth, and wild beasts, and creeping things, and fowls of the air.
>
> And I heard a voice saying unto me, Arise, Peter; slay and eat. But I said, Not so, Lord: for nothing common or unclean hath at any time entered into my mouth. But the voice answered me again from heaven, What God hath cleansed, that call not thou common. And this was done three times: and all were drawn up again into heaven. And, behold, immediately there were three men already come unto the house where I was, sent from Caesarea unto me. And the Spirit bade me go with them, nothing doubting. Moreover these six brethren accompanied me, and we entered into the man's house.

In this passage, Peter receives a different kind of vision. It was visible and audible. He was in a trance, so what he saw was not physically, but mentally, seen. In this case, the one receiving it had trouble figuring out what it meant, though it was pretty obvious.

Here is another vision, in Acts 16:9—10:

> And a vision appeared to Paul in the night; There stood a man of Macedonia, and prayed him, saying, Come over into Macedonia, and help us. And after he had seen the vision, immediately we endeavored to go into Macedonia, assuredly gathering that the Lord had called us for to preach the gospel unto them.

Here Paul receives a simple vision. This was visible and audible, though the voice was not God's. This vision was used to show God's will. The duration of the vision was not very long at all. It appears as though this vision was specifically a dream, since it was in the night.

We all have dreams now and then, but God may use dreams to communicate His will to us. You may be wondering how you can identify whether a dream is from God. As one who has experienced God-given dreams, I can answer that in four points.

First, God-given dreams are spiritually related. Second, as many God-given dreams include physical symbols with spiritual meanings, you will understand the correlation between the dream and some spiritual insight. Third, you won't forget the dream. Fourth, the more Spirit-led you are, the better you will recognize God-given dreams. Make sure you are cautious. Diligently consider whether the dream you received was truly from God, because demons can influence your mind and your dreams, and you certainly don't want to give in to their voices. Pray about the dreams you have.

Let me give another vision, found in Acts 18:9—11:

> Then spake the Lord to Paul in the night by a vision, Be not afraid, but speak, and hold not thy peace: For I am with thee, and no man shall set on thee to hurt thee: for I have much people in this city. And he continued there a year and six months, teaching the word of God among them.

Here God gives a vision to Paul (audible only) to confirm and foretell.

Second Corinthians 12:1—4 says,

> It is not expedient for me doubtless to glory. I will come to visions and revelations of the Lord. I knew a man in Christ above fourteen years ago, (whether in the body, I cannot tell; or whether out of the body, I cannot tell: God knoweth;) such an one caught up to the third heaven. And I knew such a man, (whether in the body, or out of the body, I cannot tell: God knoweth;) How that he was caught up into paradise, and heard unspeakable words, which it is not lawful for a man to utter.

In this passage, Paul tells of a vision a man he knew of received 14 years ago. For some reason, we think that he received the vision. Maybe he is referring to himself in the third person. In this vision, it was visible and audible. This man was caught up into heaven and heard voices saying things too sacred to disclose. Paul does not know whether He was in body or in spirit while he was in heaven.

Okay, so I presented quite a few visions received by men in the New Testament. They all were prepared to receive it, not doubting it was from God. It was not unexpected for God to talk to them. Why would that all-of-a-sudden change? You may say that it was because of the completion of the New Testament, but that is just an assumption. You have no good reason to believe that we don't receive visions anymore. Christians do receive visions, and I have even received visions.

Remember the prophecy in Acts 2:16—21:

> And it shall come to pass in the last days, saith God, I will pour out of my Spirit upon all flesh: and your sons and your daughters shall prophesy, and your young men shall see visions, and your old men shall dream dreams: And on my servants and on my handmaidens I will pour out in those days of my Spirit; and they shall prophesy: And I will shew wonders in heaven above, and signs in the earth beneath; blood, and fire, and vapor of smoke: The sun shall be turned into darkness, and the moon into blood, before that great and notable day of the

Why Cessationism Can't Be True

Lord come: And it shall come to pass, that whosoever shall call on the name of the Lord shall be saved.

That hasn't changed, according to Scripture. Expect visions. God is the same God who spoke to Abraham. He is the same God who spoke Daniel. He is the same God who spoke to Elijah. He is the same God who spoke to Peter. He is the same God who spoke to Paul. And He is the same God who speaks to you. He can speak through His Word, through godly counsel, through the burdening by the Holy Spirit, through His own voice, through dreams, or through trances. I hope you are willing to accept that.

That event at Pentecost was the mark of the beginning of a new age, where God's Spirit would pour out on all humanity, whoever shall call upon the name of the Lord. Whereas before, there were 400 years of silence, and before then, only certain of God's people were filled with His Spirit and received communication from God. Now, all those who call upon the name of the Lord will be filled with the Holy Spirit—sons, daughters, young men, old men, servants, and handmaidens—and will prophesy, see visions, and dream dreams.

God said that "it will come to pass in the last days." We are in the last days, so what He said about prophecies, visions, and dreams must still be true. It was not just for that generation, because He said that "your sons and your daughters shall prophesy."

Cessationists claim that all revelation from God ended when the Scriptures were complete, but just because written revelation was finished, it doesn't mean personal revelation finished. God is personal

—that is just who He is. He loves to speak to His children.

Christianity is not just looking back at a record of universal truths, and blindly following it with little experience of the God who wrote it and is written in it. Christianity is experiencing God—His works, His presence, and His voice. What happened in the book of Acts is not a monument of the Church that we look back to in admiration; it is a model of the Church that continues to this day. What is seen in Acts is what God had planned for the Church, from the first century to the last.

We are a special people, whom God blesses with wonders and miracles on a daily basis. We are the Church, where the supernatural overflows into the natural. We are the anointed, to whom God speaks with visions and dreams and revelations. God did not just leave us with His written Word in the midst of evil. He is intimately involved with His adopted children. What father just hands his child a biography of him and doesn't communicate with his child?

> Call unto me, and I will answer thee,
> and shew thee great and mighty things,
> which thou knowest not. (Jeremiah 33:3)

17

Signs, Wonders, and Miracles

I think it would be beneficial to explain the purpose and function of signs, wonders, and miracles. For some reason, Cessationists don't like the thought of its continuance. But if it has happened in the early Church age, I don't think we should be so adamant about it continuing today. Apparently, Cessationists have a stigma towards performing signs and wonders, and it would be appropriate to clarify things here.

What are signs, wonders, and miracles?

Signs, wonders, and miracles are supernatural acts that God has endowed to the Church. The Greek word for "signs" (*semeion*) literally means "an indication; characteristic; token." The Greek word for "wonders" (*teras*) means "a marvel; spectacle." The Greek word for "miracles" (*dunamis*) literally means "power; ability." These three words are often used together (or two of the three) to connote one impression: supernatural acts in the natural world intended to indicate something. "Wonders" is in reference to the audience, "miracles" is in reference to the performer, and "signs" is in reference to the connection "wonders" and "miracles" have with each other, along with their purpose. "Signs" by itself is often used to refer to "signs, wonders, and miracles." A more precise definition for "signs" would be "supernatural characteristics of the Church that display the power of God and indicate the presence of God in the Church."

What is the purpose of signs?

Signs are just that—signs. They are used to point unbelievers to the truth, the Gospel, and Jesus Christ. Any sign you see in the daily, secular life is there to point your attention to something important. A "Caution: Wet Floor" sign is there to direct your attention to the wet floor. One must note that this sign does not prove that the floor is wet. It is only if you can see that the floor is wet (which can be compared to the Holy Spirit's illumination) or until you take that step that you realize the floor is wet (which can be compared to faith). I have walked across a floor that wasn't wet, but had a "Caution: Wet Floor" sign on it. Again, a sign is there to grab your attention, not so much to prove anything.

This clarifies the common misunderstanding people can have concerning the supernatural signs done by the Church through the power of God. These signs are performed, not to prove that the Gospel is true, but to direct the attention of unbelievers to the Gospel or something else. Now, people do many times treat a sign as proof and evidence. For example, if someone looks around for an exit, and they find an exit sign, they heed to it in faith, believing it to be proof that it is indeed indicating the proper exit. But what if someone came along and replaced an entrance sign for an exit sign? That is why one must not entirely rely on signs, and this is especially the case when it comes to religion and truth.

Signs indicate many more things than just the truth and the Gospel. They indicate the presence of God in the Church or a believer (as is often the case with tongues), the love and compassion of God (as is often the case with healing), the mercy and grace of God (as is often the case with protection), the power of God (as is often the case with exorcism), and the blessing of God (as is often the case with miracles). See Psalm 103 and Psalm 136 for further elaboration. If I would sum up the function of signs and wonders in one sentence, it would be this: Signs are demonstrations of God's being and indications of God's truth. It's difficult to put an exact function on it because it has a variety of functions and purposes.

What do these signs include?

Mark 16:17—18 gives us an overview. These signs (i.e. characteristics) include:

1) Casting out demons (Acts 5:16, 8:7, 16:18, 19:12)
2) Speaking in new tongues (1 Corinthians 14:21—22)
3) Taking up serpents (Acts 28:3—6)

4) Drinking poison without being harmed (Mark 16:18)
5) Healing the sick (Acts 3:6—8, 5:15—16, 9:34, 9:40—42, 19:12, 28:8—9)
6) Prophesying (Acts 2:17—18, 19:6, 21:9)
7) And many kinds of miracles (Acts 6:8, 8:6, 8:13, 15:12)

Who can perform signs and wonders?

Every believer, through the power of the Holy Spirit can perform miracles. Mark 16:17 says that "these signs shall follow them that believe." Christ said in John 14:12,

> Verily, verily, I say unto you, He that believeth on me, the works that I do shall he do also; and greater works than these shall he do; because I go unto my Father.

Keep in mind that it is really God who performs the signs and wonders. Believers are just the instruments He uses to perform them (Acts 1:8, 2 Corinthians 4:7).

Signs are especially performed through apostles and evangelists, as is seen in the book of Acts; however, they are not the only ones who can exercise them. As is also seen in the book of Acts, Stephen (a deacon, not an apostle) performed wonders (Acts 6:8). The reason why we almost always only see the apostles performing signs in the book of Acts is because that book is specifically narrating the ministry of the first apostles in particular, not the ministry of other believers. But again, there are still apostles today, and it wasn't just the 12 Apostles and Paul who could perform signs—Barnabas also performed them (Acts 14:3).

Does the operation of signs depend on one's faith?

Apparently, it does. To operate the signs God has endowed to us, a believer must have faith that it will be performed. This is the faith that moves mountains, of which Jesus was talking about to His disciples, mentioned in Matthew 17:20 and Luke 17:6. In Matthew 17:19—20, we see that faith is needed to perform signs.

> Then came the disciples to Jesus apart, and said, Why could not we cast him out? Jesus said unto them, Because of your unbelief: for verily I say unto you, If ye have faith as a grain of mustard seed, ye shall say unto this mountain, Remove hence to yonder place; and it shall remove; and nothing shall be impossible unto you.

Sometimes, it is also dependent on the faith of the benefiter of the signs (if there is any). This is concluded by looking at Acts 14:8—10, which says,

> And there sat a certain man at Lystra, impotent in his feet, being a cripple from his mother's womb, who never had walked: The same heard Paul speak: who stedfastly beholding him, and perceiving

that he had faith to be healed, Said with
a loud voice, Stand upright on thy feet.
And he leaped and walked.

Religious critics of the faith often cannot receive the blessing of signs, wonders, and miracles. This is what Jesus indicated many times in His ministry in reference to the Pharisees (Matthew 12:38—39). However, the ministry of evangelism often includes signs and wonders because, though the people are unbelievers, God uses the miracles to demonstrate His love and power and to draw them to Him.

How are signs and wonders supposed to be exercised?

As is seen all throughout Acts, the signs and wonders are displayed first, and then the Gospel follows. Remember, signs are intended to point the audience to something, and in this case, the Gospel. We perform the sign to get the unbeliever's attention that there is something unique about us, and then we present the Gospel and tell them about Jesus, who has given us the power to perform these miracles.

We must not focus so much on the signs insomuch that we forget to share the message of truth. As a matter of fact, performing signs, wonders, and miracles is not a necessity, but rather, the preaching of God's truth. In Acts, Paul did not always demonstrate signs and wonders when he preached the Gospel, especially when he was preaching in the synagogues. Also, because signs such as healing indicate the love, compassion, and mercy of God, doing that first will open them up to the Gospel. Really, there isn't any required order structure for signs and wonders. Do whatever the Holy Spirit leads you to do.

Signs to the Jews

There is an additional purpose for signs, specifically tongues and prophesying. These signs were fulfillments of the prophecies in Isaiah 28:11—12 and Joel 2:28—32. Now, being a sign to the Jews was not the only purpose of tongues and prophecy, but an additional purpose. Yes, the Jews in the time of Acts observed the fulfillment of these prophecies, but there are still new generations of Jews today that are still to observe those fulfillments.

What about the Spirit's work in the heart?

One thing to note is that the Holy Spirit uses man to work in the heart. Really, God doesn't have to use us for anything, even for preaching the Gospel; but He has decided to use us and make us profitable. With that in mind, the Holy Spirit uses signs, wonders, and miracles to open the heart and eyes of an unbeliever. The Holy Spirit can just convict unbelievers directly and draw them to Christ, but He has, instead, decided to use a variety of different outward devices to accomplish it. This includes nature, circumstances (such as hardship), people as Christ-like examples, testimonies, and even signs and wonders.

Are signs used as authority for truth?

First, we need to discuss the word "authority." Authority for truth as "certainty" for truth would definitely not be a purpose of signs. Just because one gives a sign does not mean his message is true.

> If there arise among you a prophet, or a dreamer of dreams, and giveth thee a sign or a wonder, And the sign or the wonder come to pass, whereof he spake unto thee, saying, Let us go after other gods, which thou hast not known, and let us serve them; Thou shalt not hearken unto the words of that prophet, or that dreamer of dreams: for the LORD your God proveth you, to know whether ye love the LORD your God with all your heart and with all your soul. (Deuteronomy 13:1—3)

> And then shall that Wicked be revealed, whom the Lord shall consume with the spirit of his mouth, and shall destroy with the brightness of his coming: Even him, whose coming is after the working of Satan with all power and signs and lying wonders, And with all deceivableness of unrighteousness in them that perish; because they received not the love of the truth, that they might be saved. (2 Thessalonians 2:8—10)

> For false Christs and false prophets shall rise, and shall shew signs and wonders, to seduce, if it were possible, even the elect. (Mark 13:22)

A sign is a demonstration of power, not an authority for truth. That is why it was often debated whether a miracle was from God or from Satan (See Matthew 12:22—24, for example). In Exodus 7, when Moses turned the staff into a serpent, the sorcerers and magicians also, by the power of demons, turned their staffs into serpents. Were they too messengers of God? Quite the opposite! Signs from God showed to pagans that their false gods were nothing compared to the real and powerful God (as you can see in 1 Kings 18).

But since we are on the subject, let's talk a little about chapter 4 verses 1 through 9 in Exodus.

> And Moses answered and said, But, behold, they will not believe me, nor hearken unto my voice: for they will say, The LORD hath not appeared unto thee. And the LORD said unto him, What is that in thine hand? And he said, A rod. And he said, Cast it on the ground. And he cast it on the ground, and it became a serpent; and Moses fled from before it. And the LORD said unto Moses, Put forth thine hand, and take it by the tail. And he put forth his hand, and caught it, and it became a rod in his hand: That they may believe that the LORD God of their fathers, the God of Abraham, the

God of Isaac, and the God of Jacob, hath appeared unto thee.

And the LORD said furthermore unto him, Put now thine hand into thy bosom. And he put his hand into his bosom: and when he took it out, behold, his hand was leprous as snow. And he said, Put thine hand into thy bosom again. And he put his hand into his bosom again; and plucked it out of his bosom, and, behold, it was turned again as his other flesh. And it shall come to pass, if they will not believe thee, neither hearken to the voice of the first sign, that they will believe the voice of the latter sign. And it shall come to pass, if they will not believe also these two signs, neither hearken unto thy voice, that thou shalt take of the water of the river, and pour it upon the dry land: and the water which thou takest out of the river shall become blood upon the dry land.

It may seem as though God is implying that these signs are given as authority for truth, especially when He says, "That they may believe that the LORD God of their fathers, the God of Abraham, the God of Isaac, and the God of Jacob, hath appeared unto thee" (v. 5). We may tend to think that signs are given to confirm that what the speaker is saying is true. However, it is more correct to say that signs are given to *indicate* that what the speaker is saying is true. Notice in this passage, that God gives two more signs for Moses to do if the people do not believe him after the first one. So God is aware that one sign may not confirm what Moses is saying.

It is very important that we identify the difference between "confirmation" (i.e. authority) and "indication." With "confirmation," you don't need anything else to prove the message. Confirmation leaves no room for doubt. With "indication," however, it combines with other indications to confirm the message, and there is still a need for faith, since the message isn't entirely proven. Indication leaves room for doubt, though very little. "Indication" leads you to a conclusion, "confirmation" affirms your conclusion.

Let me illustrate this. Suppose someone told you that it was about to rain. How do you know whether to trust what they say? They show you the weather forecast (which can be compared to the Bible for this illustration), but you don't know whether to trust the weather forecast either. They then point you to the sky, and you observe the big dark clouds (which can be compared to signs and wonders). These dark clouds heavily indicate that it's going to rain, but there is still some room to doubt, because the clouds might just pass over. It is only when it actually rains that the original statement is proven, in which faith isn't necessary.

As far as signs are concerned, they do not confirm (prove; verify) truth; rather, they indicate (suggest; imply; bear witness to) truth, among other things. Remember that the Greek word for "signs" literally means "indication" (as we discussed earlier). Because signs are not a confirmation of truth, God gave Moses the power to perform additional signs in case the Israelites did not believe him at the first sign.

> But though he had done so many miracles before them, yet they believed not on him. (John 12:37)

Now consider that in relation to the New Testament Church. God has allowed us to perform signs so as to indicate to the world that God is real and that Christianity is not just any other religion. Just like nature indicates the existence of God, the signs and wonders displayed by the Church indicate that God is with them and is of the truth, and to leave no room for excuse (John 15:24).

Consider Hebrews 2:4, which says,

> How shall we escape, if we neglect so great salvation; which at the first began to be spoken by the Lord, and was confirmed unto us by them that heard him; God also bearing them witness, both with signs and wonders, and with divers miracles, and gifts of the Holy Ghost, according to his own will?

The Greek word used for "bearing them witness" means, according to Strong's Greek Dictionary, "to testify further jointly, that is, unite in adding evidence." You can see how the signs were not a sole proof, but further indications or evidences.

> But when the Comforter is come, whom I will send unto you from the Father, even the Spirit of truth, which proceedeth from the Father, he shall testify of me. (John15:26)

Here, the Greek word for "testify" is actually related to the Greek word in Hebrews 2:4, which means to "also bear witness." When Christ said that the Holy Spirit would testify of Him, He was probably also considering the signs and wonders that the Spirit would display through the Church to testify of Him.

What about Mark 16:20? It says,

> And they went forth, and preached everywhere, the Lord working with them, and confirming the word with signs following.

What about Hebrews 2:3? It says,

> How shall we escape, if we neglect so great salvation; which at the first began to be spoken by the Lord, and was confirmed unto us by them that heard him.

The Greek word for "confirm" literally means "to establish; stabilitate." This does not reference proof, but rather, strengthening—something gradual, like reinforcement. There are other Greek words used to mean "to prove" (see Acts 24:13 and Acts 25:7).

Still Continuing

Mark 16:15—18 says,

> And he said unto them, Go ye into all the world, and preach the gospel to every creature. He that believeth and is baptized shall be saved; but he that

> believeth not shall be damned. And these signs shall follow them that believe; In my name shall they cast out devils; they shall speak with new tongues; They shall take up serpents; and if they drink any deadly thing, it shall not hurt them; they shall lay hands on the sick, and they shall recover.

All Christ has said here applies today. As long as we are still called to preach the Gospel, we are still called to perform signs and wonders by the power of God.

John 14:12—14 says,

> Verily, verily, I say unto you, He that believeth on me, the works that I do shall he do also; and greater works than these shall he do; because I go unto my Father. And whatsoever ye shall ask in my name, that will I do, that the Father may be glorified in the Son. If ye shall ask any thing in my name, I will do it.

Just as God said that whoever believes will be saved, so He said that whoever believes will do the works that Christ did (including miracles). What's more, Christ promises that the Father will do whatever we ask of Him if we ask in the name of Jesus. This means that if we ask for healing in the name of Jesus, the Father will heal. This means that if we beseech God to cast out a demon in the name of Jesus, He will do it. Now, He does say elsewhere that it must be done in faith (e.g. Matthew 17:14—21).

John 3:1—2 says,

> There was a man of the Pharisees, named Nicodemus, a ruler of the Jews: The same came to Jesus by night, and said unto him, Rabbi, we know that thou art a teacher come from God: for no man can do these miracles that thou doest, except God be with him.

If doing those miracles Jesus did meant that God was with Him, then wouldn't that mean that if God is with us, we can do those miracles? After all, Jesus is Emmanuel, "God with Us."

We have a similar case in Acts 10:37—38:

> That word, I say, ye know, which was published throughout all Judaea, and began from Galilee, after the baptism which John preached; How God anointed Jesus of Nazareth with the Holy Ghost and with power: who went about doing good, and healing all that were oppressed of the devil; for God was with him.

Notice at the end of this text that the reason Jesus could heal all that were oppressed was not because He was God (though He was), but because God was with Him. Jesus came as a man (though still inherently being God) and even left His right to divine glory and power, yet He still could do the miraculous. That is because God was with Him.

The encouraging truth concerning this is that God is with us just as He was with our Savior! Jesus set the example for us to follow. He showed to us by his life and ministry what our potential is. Notice also that in the beginning of verse 38, it says that God anointed Jesus with the Holy Ghost and with power. And we too have been anointed with the Holy Ghost and with power (Acts 1:8)! Wouldn't that mean we can do the same things Christ did?

Nowhere in Scripture does it say that signs, wonders, and miracles were only for the early Church. God intended for them to continue throughout the ages of the Church, to point the world to the Gospel of Jesus Christ. There is no problem with it unless you create one. Scripture allows it to continue, and they have continued. The Church has been displaying signs and wonders through the power of the Spirit for centuries, from Pentecost to now. It is a tool of the Spirit, and an instrument of the Gospel. It leads people to Christ. It shows to the world that "the kingdom of God is not in word, but in power" (1 Corinthians 4:20).

18

Why Cessationists Are Still Cessationists

I will not be surprised if some Cessationists, after reading this, will continue believing and teaching Cessationism. Why? If it is clearly unbiblical, why would they still hold onto that view? The answer is the answer for why all believers of false doctrine continue believing it even when presented with clear evidence against it. The simple answer can be wrapped up in one word: Tradition.

They have been taught it to begin with, they have believed it since the past, and may have even taught it in the past. Sometimes it is a belief they have come to grasp by their own way. They hesitate to give up a belief they have had for a while, since it characterizes them and their perspective. They don't want to change their perspective or lifestyle, so they hesitate to give up a traditional belief of theirs.

It's hard to give up tradition. Whether you were once an Atheist, Buddhist, Muslim, Hinduist, or some other idol worshipper, it took great faith to step out of that darkness and into the light of Christianity. Many remain in their religion because of tradition. What a person considers to be the truth tends to be the religion or belief they have been raised in. Tradition is the number one obstacle to truth. Within Christianity, usually those raised in Baptist churches remain Baptists, those raised in Reformed churches remain reformed, those raised in Pentecostal churches remain Pentecostal, those raised in Lutheran churches remain Lutheran, those raised in Methodist churches remain Methodist, etc.

Are you beginning to see why Cessationists are still Cessationists? They want to remain faithful. They want to remain strong. They want to remain persistent. They want to remain consistent. The problem is, however, that they are doing all of that with a false teaching. Instead of what we traditionally have believed, we must be faithful to the Word, strong in the Word, persistent in the Word, and consistent with the Word. If it is on behalf of God's Word, we must reject any traditional beliefs.

I believe another major cause for the continuation of Cessationism, despite the major valid arguments against the belief, is because they are prideful (not wanting to admit their error) and they are prejudiced. If you are a Cessationist, let me ask you this question: Why do you want to believe these gifts ceased? What do you have against people speaking in tongues, prophesying, working miracles, and healing people? Why are you so careful not to admit those gifts do still exist? You certainly do not have a biblical reason! Is there anything wrong with accepting the fact that they do still exist? Now I know I'm assuming they are prejudiced, but think about it: Why do Cessationists try so desperately to defend a belief that really isn't biblical?

I believe that because these "sign gifts" and "revelatory

Why Cessationism Can't Be True

gifts" are unique and supernatural, Cessationists want to believe that it is too good to be true that they do still exist. But it did happen in the past, so why can't it still happen today? Also, notice that every Cessationist does not have those gifts (at least those that are noticeable: tongues, prophecy, miracles, and healings). "Uh, Of course!" you may say. But think about it: everyone who has those gifts *know* that the gifts do still exist, because it exists in them, and they experience it. I bet you that if a Cessationist was given one of those gifts, he would no longer be a Cessationist. Really, it's obvious that Cessationists have a prejudice deep down inside them, because they simply just don't want to admit that the gifts do still exist.

Another reason is because of the problems they see in many of the Charismatic churches. They don't want to associate with the chaos. And some, unfortunately, don't want to be involved in the "over-excitement" of spiritual worship. They feel like bringing the gifts back into the church will cause the worship services to become informal. They have come to be too comfortable with the formality of the church services. But were the "services" in the New Testament age formal?

Some may not want to abandon their belief in Cessationism because they have taught it so diligently, wrote and published books defending it, and don't want to waste all that work and effort. Also, if they change, then (if they are a pastor or spiritual leader) the congregations will not know whether to trust whether the other things they teach are true. Additionally, they fear that they will cause division in their churches and cause many to look down on them.

Such a change in doctrine will definitely change the life of the church, with other gifts being brought back in. A lot of pastors don't want to even think about changing their theology on this issue because they don't want any dramatic change in the life of the church. It even feels kind of "unorthodox" to them. It may feel weird and uncomfortable because you are not used to it (kind of like a culture shock), but that is what the original Church of our Lord was like. Let go of tradition, and let go of your prejudices for the sake of the Church and the truth.

The root problem with Cessationism and why it is so hard to let go of it is that their mindset and perspective is wrong when it comes to Christianity. They forget that God is the same God of the Old Testament Israelites and the early apostles. They forget that the kingdom of God does not just consist of talk, but also of power (1 Corinthians 4:20). They forget that God thought it good to give us power, blessings, and privileges through His Holy Spirit. They have the false notion that the Church today is not the same as it was in the early New Testament age. That is completely absurd! Why would they ever assume that? The New Testament continues to us today, and applies to us today—all of it. That includes all the signs, gifts, and visions. God gave those gifts and signs to the Church with the intention that they will continue with the Church. We are the same Church as the early Church, and nothing is different today than in the early centuries of the Church.

It may not even be anything to do with tradition. It may be their experience that leads them to conclude that the miraculous gifts and signs do not continue to exist. They don't see it being done in person, so they become skeptics. But one must not elevate experience above God's Word.

19

It Makes a Difference

Does it really matter what we believe regarding the gifts of the Spirit? There are doctrines that really are not that important. First Timothy 1:4 says,

> Neither give heed to fables and endless genealogies, which minister questions, rather than godly edifying which is in faith.

Second Timothy 2:23 says,

> But foolish and unlearned questions avoid, knowing that they do gender strifes.

Titus 3:9 says,

> But avoid foolish questions, and genealogies, and contentions, and strivings about the law; for they are unprofitable and vain.

Is the subject of Cessationism an unnecessary

debate? Not at all! Much attention should be put to this matter. It makes a huge difference.

The first reason is because God commands these gifts to be used. If you believe you don't have to follow those commands anymore, you must have good reason to believe that. If Cessationism is not true, what would you say to God when He judges your obedience? You have no explicit Scripture as a defense. What you believe about the gifts is a matter of obedience and disobedience. Isn't it preferred that you obey God, unless God clearly nullifies the command?

The second reason is because it has to do with what the Holy Spirit does and does not do. Who are you to determine what the Spirit does not do anymore? Did God tell you that some of the gifts are not being given anymore? No. You have come up with that idea on your own accord. The Holy Spirit can do what He wants.

> But all these worketh that one and the selfsame Spirit, dividing to every man severally as *he will.*" (1 Corinthians 12:11)

It appears as though Cessationists are stepping into the shoes of the Pharisees, who accused Jesus of performing miracles through the power of demons. Cessationists accuse Charismatics of performing miracles through the power of demons. Isn't that a risky move? This is a serious accusation.

Matthew 12:22—32 records,

> Then was brought unto him one possessed with a devil, blind, and dumb: and he healed him, insomuch that the blind and

dumb both spake and saw. And all the people were amazed, and said, Is not this the son of David? But when the Pharisees heard it, they said, This fellow doth not cast out devils, but by Beelzebub the prince of the devils.

And Jesus knew their thoughts, and said unto them, Every kingdom divided against itself is brought to desolation; and every city or house divided against itself shall not stand: And if Satan cast out Satan, he is divided against himself; how shall then his kingdom stand? And if I by Beelzebub cast out devils, by whom do your children cast them out? therefore they shall be your judges.

But if I cast out devils by the Spirit of God, then the kingdom of God is come unto you. Or else how can one enter into a strong man's house, and spoil his goods, except he first bind the strong man? and then he will spoil his house. He that is not with me is against me; and he that gathereth not with me scattereth abroad.

Wherefore I say unto you, All manner of sin and blasphemy shall be forgiven unto men: but the blasphemy against the Holy Ghost shall not be forgiven unto men. And whosoever speaketh a word against the Son of man, it shall be forgiven him: but whosoever speaketh against the

> Holy Ghost, it shall not be forgiven him, neither in this world, neither in the world to come.

It is dangerous to claim that the works performed by Charismatics are not being done by the Spirit, but by demons. How are they so certain? They are relying on speculation and questionable handling of Scripture. They are walking on shaky and hazardous ground.

The third reason is that it deals with the church itself. Remember the unity and cooperation of the gifts explained in 1 Corinthians 12. What you believe regarding the gifts makes a big difference in church life. This matter affects the church directly. It determines the effectiveness of the church and the liveliness of the church. You are missing out if, in fact, Cessationism is not true.

I am not just rambling on and on about some stupid and pointless debate. This is a serious matter. Cessationism is a dangerous disease that cripples the Church. The truth in this matter makes a huge difference that significantly affects the Church. I will talk more about that in the next book, titled "What Cessationism Has Done to the Church."

Conclusion

The U.S. Constitution is a series of articles and amendments that provide the federal laws of the United States. In 1919, the Constitution ratified the prohibition of the sale, distribution, and consumption of alcoholic beverages. Is it still prohibited today? No! How do you know? Is it because you see many people selling it and drinking it? No! It's because you saw it in the Constitution!

Now, we know that selling, distributing, and consuming alcoholic beverages is legal, but let's say that no one was selling it or drinking it. You begin to scratch your head. "Did alcoholic beverages become prohibited?" you ask yourself. Then you determine that it has become prohibited.

You come across a man who is drinking alcohol, and you reprimand him. "Don't drink that! It's illegal!"

He replies, "That's not true! The Constitution never prohibited it again."

You respond, "But don't you see how that in the recent past no one sold it or drank it anymore? Also, everyone I know who drinks alcohol has been put in jail."

The man answers back. "There were still people who drank and sold alcohol in the recent past. The ones who were put in jail were convicted for drunk driving or some other felony, not for drinking. We can drink alcohol; we just can't drive while we are drunk."

The Bible does not prohibit the "sign gifts." Sure, it may have appeared that they have ceased after the "Apostolic Age," and there may be a lot of problems that are associated with the gifts; but, that doesn't mean those gifts are prohibited. There are abuses that can occur in Charismatic circles, but it is not the gifts that are the problem—it is the abuse of the gifts. Remember, just as we can't say that an amendment of the Constitution doesn't apply anymore unless there is another amendment that nullifies it, we can't say that certain gifts of the Holy Spirit don't apply anymore unless there is Scripture that nullifies it.

The conclusion is this: Cessationism is not true. It can't be true. It has no genuine scriptural support. Nowhere in the Bible does it say that the "sign gifts" have ceased or will cease when the Scriptures are completed. The term "sign gifts" was invented by man, and the idea that some of the gifts of the Spirit have ceased to be given anymore was invented purely by man with his human reasoning and logic. It may have appeared as though certain gifts have ceased, since they haven't seen any believer with any of those gifts; however, that does not mean that those gifts have ceased.

The arguments Cessationists present as a defense for their belief are only *reasons for* their belief, not *proofs of* their belief. In other words, their arguments are good for showing why or how their belief can be true, but their arguments don't show that it is true. If Cessationism were true, Cessationists could use their arguments to explain how the doctrine makes sense.

But they have nothing as a foundation to validate their doctrine.

Let's be open, willing, and subject to the Scriptures. We must not master the Bible; instead, we should be mastered by the Bible. Remember, our foundation is the Word of God. So if we begin to dismiss biblical evidence and form our own evidence, we are subduing the only secure foundation—that is, Christ and His Word.

So let's be completely open to the truth. There are 4 basic faults in the Cessationist's view: it is unbiblical, it uses erroneous exegesis to have scriptural support, it is defended with prejudice, and it is held on to in the name of tradition. In addition to those 4 faults, there are 5 basic proofs that the gifts do still exists: Scripture says they are necessary, Scripture indicates they are normative, Scripture says they will end when we are glorified, Scripture commands that they be used and accepted, and (I should at least get one evidence outside of Scripture) the gifts are still being given to and used by genuine Christians.

One thing I realized is that Cessationism is the doctrine of exceptions. In other words, they affirm spiritual truths with the exception of the sign gifts. Permit me to give examples of this.

1) They affirm that we are to follow the footsteps of Jesus, except for doing the miracles He did.
2) They affirm that what Jesus told His disciples in the Gospels apply to us as well, except for when he told them to "heal the sick, cleanse the lepers, raise the dead, cast out devils" (Matthew 10:8).

3) They affirm that all that God commands in the New Testament apply to us today, except for His commands to heal the sick, not despise prophesyings, desire to prophesy, and not forbid speaking in tongues.
4) They affirm that all the gifts are equally necessary in the body of Christ, except for the "sign gifts."
5) They affirm that God still gives the gifts mentioned in Romans 12, 1 Corinthians 12, and Ephesians 4 to the Church, except for the sign gifts.
6) They affirm that the book of Acts is a guide for the Church today, except in reference to the signs and wonders that were done.
7) They affirm that all God's promises (at least in the New Testament) remain true for us today, except His promise to heal those whom we lay hands on (James 5:15), grant whatever we ask in faith (Mark 11:24), and perform signs through us (Mark 16:17—18).
8) They affirm that God still provides the Church with spiritual leaders as mentioned in Ephesians 4, except apostles and prophets.
9) They affirm that the giving out of the spiritual gifts will cease when the end of time arrives, except for those sign gifts.
10) They affirm that God has performed miracles through His servants in every age, except for this age.
11) They affirm that every doctrine we teach must be based on Scripture alone, except for the doctrine of Cessationism (and maybe some others).

There are probably more, but you should get the point by now. What is there to resist? God didn't tell you to forbid these gifts, and He didn't tell you these gifts ceased; so therefore, you have permission to accept these gifts as still being given to Christians. If God didn't say, then nothing's changed. God didn't say that these gifts ceased, so they haven't. God's Word stands. That's all we need to be assured that the gifts have not ceased.

If I had to give only one theological summary concerning the issue, it would be this: Either you accept all the gifts for today, or you reject them all entirely. You can't cherry-pick which ones you think or feel have ceased or continued. Paul did not categorize the gifts. He laid them out, with "sign gifts" being intermingled with the other gifts. His lists weren't even exhaustive lists—they were just the surface of the manifold gifts and blessings of God! I could make just as good of a case for the cessation of all the spiritual gifts, if not better. But the intention of the gifts of God were not for temporarily helping us until the Scriptures were completed—that can't be found anywhere in Scripture! They were gifts, not aids or tools. The gifts were given so that we can have the privilege of profiting, perfecting, and edifying the body of Christ (1 Corinthians 12:7, Ephesians 4:7—12).

If you want to continue to believe in Cessationism, just don't be falsely informing others that the gifts have ceased. And just realize that you are believing a lie and are disobeying God. But the truth stands: the Holy Spirit gives varyingly to the children of God the gifts of wisdom, knowledge, faith, healings, working of miracles, prophecy, discernment of spirits, speaking in tongues, interpretation of tongues, apostleship, pastoralship, teaching, helping, administration, exhortation, generosity, leadership, mercifulness, etc. (Romans 12:6—8, 1 Corinthians 12:8—10, 28); and none of these have ceased to be given to the saints of God. Let me end with this verse:

"Add thou not unto his words, lest he reprove thee, and thou be found a liar" (Proverbs 30:8).